SCEPTICISM AND DOGMA

A Study in the Philosophy of F. H. Bradley

BY
RALPH GILBERT ROSS

SCEPTICISM AND DOGMA

SCEPTICISM AND DOGMA

A Study in the Philosophy of F. H. Bradley

BY

RALPH GILBERT ROSS, Ph.D.
Instructor in Philosophy
University of Newark

NEW YORK
1940

COPYRIGHT, 1940, BY RALPH GILBERT ROSS
Manufactured in the United States of America

TO MY MOTHER AND FATHER, IN LOVE AND ADMIRATION.

ABBREVIATIONS

AR—APPEARANCE AND REALITY, Oxford, 1930.
TR—ESSAYS ON TRUTH AND REALITY, Oxford, 1914.
CE—COLLECTED ESSAYS, Oxford, 1935.
PL—PRINCIPLES OF LOGIC, Oxford, 1928.

ACKNOWLEDGMENTS

One of the advantages of publication is the opportunity it affords for expressing publicly one's intellectual debts. It would be pleasant to estimate the influence on the following pages of those thinkers of the past who have seemed most instructive; but that would be mere confession, not thanks. And I should like here to thank those who have, in one manner or another, aided me in this study.

Professor M. R. Schneck, of the University of Arizona, awakened me to the value and power of systematic enquiry and rigorous analysis. Dean Emil R. Riesen, also of the University of Arizona, clarified, by his teaching and example, the meaning of those practical goals which are the uses of philosophy. To both of them I am deeply grateful.

In the actual preparation of this essay I was helped enormously by numerous conversations with Professor Ernest Nagel, of Columbia University, to whom I am indebted for friendly advice and incisive criticism. I am sensible, also, of my debt to Professor John Herman Randall, Jr., whose brilliant lectures on Bradley I attended, and of a special debt to Professor Frederick J. E. Woodbridge, whose penetration and insight into the history and problems of philosophy were a source of constant inspiration and delight.

These acknowledgments would not be complete if I did not express thanks to Professor Herbert W. Schneider, Professor Harry A. Overstreet, and Professor Sidney Hook for their encouragement and friendship.

RALPH GILBERT ROSS

New York City
April 1, 1940

TABLE OF CONTENTS

Chapter One: Introduction 7

Chapter Two: Logic
                   1. General Remarks 13
                   2. Judgment and Idea 15
                   3. Modality 20
                   4. Inference 24
                   5. Judgment and Inference 27
                   6. Judgment, Inference and Truth 29

Chapter Three: Logic—Terminal Essays
                   1. Inference 47
                   2. Judgment 53
                   3. The Negative Judgment 66

Chapter Four: Appearance
                   1. Introductory 75
                   2. Relation and Quality 80

Chapter Five: Appearance and Reality
                   1. The Criterion (I) 93
                   2. Levels of Reality 100
                   3. The Criterion (II) 108

Chapter Six: Three Theories of Truth
                   1. Points of View and Theories of Truth   112
                   2. "Floating Ideas" and Error 120

Chapter Seven: The Ideal and the Real
                   1. The Ideal, The Real, and Satisfaction .. 123
                   2. Appearance, Idea, and Relation 131

Chapter Eight: Scepticism and Dogma 144

Chapter Nine: Conclusion 152

SCEPTICISM AND DOGMA
A Study in the Philosophy of F. H. Bradley

CHAPTER I
INTRODUCTION

A man who demands satisfactory evidence for any contention will find that there are many things he cannot believe, but he will preserve towards those propositions for which the evidence is not sufficient an attitude of tolerant agnosticism. Disbelief, or the denial of the truth of a statement, will require evidence as conclusive as the assertion of its truth. For such a man scepticism, which asserts the inability to know certain things, is in the same class as any other assertion or denial. Belief in it is based on the support of sufficient relevant evidence, and without that evidence a man's belief loses its rational character.

Scepticism as a philosophical doctrine both denies and asserts. It denies that man can know some kind of thing and it makes this denial on the basis of a positive limit which it asserts of knowledge. The evidence it advances must, on this account, be within the field of epistemology; and it must be gathered by the use of some technique. If one examines the presuppositions and technique of a skeptic, he will find a scepticism already implicit in them, even though an avowedly sceptical method is not followed. The sceptical judgments which can be extracted from the statement of Locke's starting point, for example, are such that they must yield sceptical conclusions, whereas the explicitly sceptical method used by Descartes does not necessarily arrive at any such ultimate denials of knowledge. In the case of the Cartesian philosophy, rather dubious principles of construction are introduced (as, for example, the contention that God would not deceive M. Descartes) but even without them non-sceptical conclusions can be reached.

So scepticism is both a method in epistemology and a conclusion of epistemology. In the first case it reveals a technique for studying the objects of knowledge; in the second case it denies that certain entities can ever be objects of knowledge. And it is important to inquire how far such a denial can go. Perhaps the best example of extreme scepticism which is still rational can be found in David Hume. Matter and self are both denied but there is no question of denying phenomena. Even if the whole world were merely a dream, as both Calderon and Shakespeare intimated, it would be nonsense to deny that there is a dream. Predicate of the world what you like! Call it material and independent, say it is spiritual and mind-dependent, assert that it is fiction, illusion, or dream; the subject-matter, the world, cannot be denied. And, on the basis of the ways in which it is known, and different portions are known in different ways, one can pass from epistemology to ontology and attempt to determine the status in being of different kinds of entities. I know things about a tree in one way, about Julius Caesar in another, and about the law of contradiction in a third. The ways in which they are known yield knowledge of the kinds of things they are and definitions of such words as "existence" must ultimately be formulated in terms of the ways in which such fields *can* be known, whether or not they actually *are* known at any time. When one predicates existence of an object he may be adding no new terms to the way in which it is defined but he is saying that a certain type of proposition containing this object as subject term can be verified empirically. Or if "existence" is taken as a field, it is that field whose content can be experienced sensuously, propositions within which can be verified in one way rather than another. But there must be more to our investigation. We must examine the things of which we are aware, in themselves, analyzing them without any reference, for it would be irrelevant, to the mind which examines. "Not the nature of consciousness, but the data of consciousness, are what the critic must fall back upon in the last resort; and Hume had been in this respect a more penetrating critic than Kant."[1]

In the examination of knowledge, the philosopher should be concerned with the ways in which things are presented to consciousness, not with the structure of consciousness itself. The latter is an independent investigation interesting in itself but irrelevant to the objects of consciousness. Many critics, I am sure, would object to such statements. Does not a study of consciousness and of mind teach us how much of what we know is purely a mental construction and how much is an independent existence; does it not reveal to what extent things are altered or modified in becoming objects of knowledge? The answer

---

[1] Santayana, Character and Opinion in the United States, p. 147.

and what is the "I" all through this discussion? Mr. R.'s body?

consists in making a distinction between two separate investigations. In one we are concerned with the objects of knowledge and the manner in which judgments about them are formulated. The paper on which I am writing can become an object of knowledge. I look at it, feel it, even taste it; I apply a match to a similar piece and immerse still another in water. I can perform a great number of experiments upon it. My conclusions are stated in a series of propositions in which meaning is contained by virtue of the use of relations. But I know still other things about the paper. I know of what material it is made and what the process of manufacture is. This is information I have acquired from others who originally gathered it in a manner similar to my own observations.

There are other things I know in different ways. My knowledge of geologic eras is based on inferences from types of rock structure and the paleontological data contained in them. I know the Pythagorean theorem but my knowledge is of a different kind from that about the paper. Finally, I know that the Pythagorean theorem and these sheets of paper are different kinds of entities. And my evidence is that they are known and used in different kinds of ways.

If I turn to an examination of mind I must first ask myself what it is that I am examining. Suppose I call it that which knows. It may be the body that knows and my investigation becomes one of physiology and physiological psychology. In this case I can proceed to investigate the body as I investigated the paper. But it may be something else that knows and if it is, and is beyond any kind of observation, then, since it is certainly not an entity like those of mathematics and logic, how am I going to know anything about it? If I assume its existence I might at least know how it functions. It functions to produce knowledge. So the only way to learn anything about it is to return to the first type of investigation and give up the second altogether. I should be suspicious of any such entity in any event. If it be called a power, then the only way to learn anything about it would be to examine what it does. And if it be called a real entity in which it is necessary to believe in order to explain knowledge, I think it would be easy enough to offer a much simpler explanation of knowledge, viz. there is a physical organism called the body and one of its functions is knowing. In any event, define the mind as you will, say anything you can about its structure—it is not in any way relevant to the examination of knowledge.

When we turn to a rational scepticism, however, we are confronted by one of the most vital tendencies of modern thought. The prestige of science has contributed greatly to making "scepticism" an honorific term and in opposing it sharply to "dogma." Scepticism, as it has functioned in the history of philosophy, has little to do with so simple a dichotomy. In more sophisticated thinkers scepticism is never kept completely apart from dogma of one kind or another; one can even point to any given rule of scientific procedure as itself a methodological dogma. Themes of scepticism and dogma are many and varied, presenting aspects of a problem which might be greatly clarified by successive analyses of different relations between the two as found in historic philosophies.

Dogma may be defined in various ways, no one of which, perhaps, gives the full flavor of the word. The axioms within a purely deductive system might be regarded as dogmatic since no evidence is offered in their behalf within the system itself, although within the framework of some other system they might be demonstrated, in terms of still other axioms. Techniques and rules of procedure might be regarded as methodological dogmas, since any evidence of their validity within the system in which they function can be gathered and presented only in terms of the rules themselves. On the other hand, it is common to mean by dogma the unsupported voice of authority or tradition. My use of the word in connection with Bradley will be, in general, to regard as dogma all doctrines about actual or possible experience which are concerned with more than its formal structure, or categories, and which are justified solely or chiefly by a dialectic, based perhaps on such things as essences, the abstract structure of thought, the aspirations of mankind, or the will of God, rather than on an appeal to the empirical itself. And I hope that, as I use the term, it will contain no evaluative element, honorific or deprecatory.

That one man, within the limitations of a system of philosophy, can appear before the reader first in the role of sceptic, then in the role of dogmatist, and finally in a dual role as both, is a phenomenon worthy of understanding. Such a man was Francis Herbert Bradley, one of the most profound of modern sceptics, who was at the same time an absolutist in systematic philosophy. Just how and in what respects Bradley was both these things, it is the purpose of this inquiry to discover.

It will be my contention that the first book of *Appearance and Reality,* which is entitled *Appearance,* is characterized by the use of a sceptical method, resulting in the denial of the ultimate validity as principles of explanation of all categories an understanding of which involves the concept of relation; and that Bradley's metaphysics is based upon the validity of that which is not denied by an application of his criterion. These considerations may be taken as having generated my inquiry, which will be concerned with the formation of Bradley's criterion from the doctrine, worked out in detail in *The Principles of Logic*, that idea, judgment, and inference constitute a system such that every part is dependent upon every other part and upon the whole, both for its meaning and its truth. Then I shall try to show how the criterion functions in Bradley's metaphysics to produce ultimate affirmations, or dogma, and ultimate denials of man's ability to know, or scepticism. It would be interesting to use the same technique to investigate Bradley's ethics and his psychology but that is not, at the moment, relevant to this undertaking. Finally, it is my hope that, in the course of this inquiry, some light may be shed on the meaning of Bradley's system as a whole.

The interpretation of Bradley at which I shall arrive will picture him as an Idealist whose philosophy, up to a point, is similar to that of the New Realists. I shall not, however, minimize the importance of the Absolute in his system. As I understand it, belief in a Whole which transcends ordinary experience is essential to the structure of his argument. Here I differ with Professor Rudolf Kagey, who has argued his case most persuasively in *The Growth of F. H. Bradley's Logic*. The nature of my disagreement will, I hope, be made clear in my concluding chapter. At this point, however, I should like to say that I follow Professor Kagey in thinking that the differences between Bradley and his non-Idealistic contemporaries have been much over-emphasized. The actual differences, which are perhaps chiefly those of approach and temper are, however, very important.

The spirit in which Bradley set out, the object of his writing as he understood it, is quite clear. "We want no system-making or systems home-grown or imported. This life-breath of persons who write about philosophy is not the atmosphere where philosophy lives. What we want at present is to clear the ground, so that English Philosophy, if it rises, may not be choked by prejudice. The ground can not be cleared without a critical or, if you prefer it, a sceptical study of first principles."[2] This he says in 1883; and in 1893 he still sees the need for "a sceptical study of first principles"—he repeats the phrase—but, the ground being clear, he knows what must follow and is eager to make the attempt. "The chief need of English philosophy is, I think, a sceptical study of first principles. . . . By scepticism is not meant doubt about or disbelief in some tenet or tenets. I understand by it an attempt to become aware of and to doubt all preconceptions. Such scepticism is the result only of labor and education, but it is a

---

[2] *PL,* p. x.

training which cannot with impunity be neglected. And I know no reason why the English mind, if it would but subject itself to this discipline, should not in our day produce a rational system of first principles."[3] It is the consequences of these statements that I propose to examine.

The only excuse I have to offer for my prefatory remarks on the nature of scepticism is that it is far better to make explicit the grounds on which any criticism I make must rest than to multiply difficulties for the reader by making remarks which must, in any event, imply those very views. And I think that, in doing this, I am proceeding in a spirit which does no violence to the temper of F. H. Bradley.

---

[3] *AR,* p. x.

CHAPTER II

LOGIC

1. GENERAL REMARKS

I. It seems evident that the two chief sections of *Appearance and Reality* are the consequences of an attempt by Bradley to satisfy what he calls in his preface "the chief need of English Philosophy"—"a sceptical study of first principles"—and then the production, on the basis of what has been learned, or what doctrines have been unlearned, of "a rational system of first principles." In the chapters which fall under the heading of *Appearance* Bradley employs the method of scepticism in the consideration of many of the traditional problems of philosophy. Exactly what he means by scepticism is made clear in the same paragraph in his preface, which has already been quoted in full. Scepticism is "an attempt to become aware of and to doubt all preconceptions." Thought, however, being what it is, the preconceptions which a man doubts will be dependent on the preconceptions, or principles, if that seems a fairer word here, which that man already believes. All criticism, Bradley contended, rests on a ground and to attack any opinion is to imply, by the substance of one's attack, a position from which it is launched. So Bradley would be the first, it seems, to insist that his own sceptical onslaught was dominated, in the selection of its victims as well as in the manner of their destruction, by principles at which he had already arrived and which had become an integral portion of his manner of thinking.

II. There is little difficulty in discovering where these principles are expounded. In his earlier work, *The Principles of Logic,* he forges the intellectual tools with which he works in the field of metaphysics and which, in turn, are refined and sharpened by his conclusions in that field. In his logical studies he is already embarked on the analysis of the metaphysical problems which were to emerge as his chief preoccupation. For one who treats logic as a formal discipline devoid of ontological significance it is possible to discuss alternate systems of logic, like alternate systems of chess, in terms of their structures and principles of operation; for one who, like Bradley, thinks of logic as one system it is usual to treat it as though it has some intimate relation to the nature of the "real", or of "experience", whatever those terms mean to the thinker concerned. That Bradley attempts to avoid metaphysical questions as much as he can in his treatment of logic but that he is sure that logical problems constantly raise metaphysical issues, is a commonplace to readers of *The Principles of Logic*. In the *Preface to First Edition* he mentions that his consideration of logic has taken him into metaphysics: "In conclusion I may be allowed to anticipate two criticisms which will be passed on my work. One reader will lament that he is overdone with Metaphysics, while another will stand on his right to have far more. I would assure the first that I have stopped where I could, and as soon as I was able. And in answer to the second I can only plead that my metaphysics are really very limited. This does not mean that, like more gifted writers, I verify in my own shortcomings the necessary defects of the human reason. It means that, on all questions, if you push me far enough, at present I end in doubts and perplexities. And on this account at least no lover of metaphysics will judge of me hardly. Still in the end perhaps both objectors are right. If I saw further I should be simpler. But I doubt if either would then be less dissatisfied."[1]

It seems, then, that Bradley's logical investigations are not to be regarded as special inquiries into a technical field, having little or no relation to the main body of his work, but, on the contrary, as an integral portion of his general philosophy. This might be more than a little puzzling if the manipulation of symbols were the essence of Bradley's investigations; but this is not the case. Bradley is part of a long tradition which regards logic as establishing fundamental principles of ontology. And, as I shall try to show later, logic, for Bradley, is as much an examination of the real as is metaphysics. The very titles of his chapters (like those of Bosanquet's) might more readily be classified to-day as topics in the philosophy of logic, or in the theory of knowledge, rather than in logic itself. And there is an important connection between such a subject matter and the consequences of employing the sceptical method.

Basically, it is the nature of inference that is at issue, its operations and its elements: judgments and terms, or ideas. The question of where thinking takes its start or, indeed, if it does take its start anywhere and how far it can go, taking its origin in one kind of material rather than another, presupposes a rather detailed theory of inference. Such problems as the validity of the ontological argument and the possibility of synthetic propositions a priori have, as their solutions, some consequence of a consideration of judgment and inference.[2] And when

---
[1] p. x.
[2] E.g., the belief that on the basis of "self-evident truths" one can deduce propositions about existence, usually presupposes that empirical propositions can be inferred from analytic propositions.

the sceptical method is used it may be reinforced by a theory of inference which helps make clear why certain presuppositions are open to doubt, being based, perhaps, on a type of inference which is permissible only of some other kind of subject matter; or the method, after fastening attention on the datum or on immediate experience, may be complemented by conclusions as to the nature of inference which aid in determining whether it is possible to transcend the given inferentially. It is the latter use of a theory of inference which enables a thinker, whose use of the sceptical method culminates in a consideration of the datum, to evade the obvious and to forego empirical philosophy for the pleasures of Absolutism or the lesser raptures of rationalist metaphysics sans Absolute. In the case of Descartes, whose use of the method of scepticism is the classical example, it is only because he believed that a certain use of inference was legitimate that he could pass so rapidly from one of his own thoughts as a datum to the existence of God.

The importance which I have attributed to judgment and inference in an enterprise such as Bradley's is not only implicit in the nature of the argument and obvious from the chapter headings of *The Principles of Logic* but is explicitly avowed by the author himself; in writing of the character of logic, he states: "Its direct and primary purpose is . . . to set out the general essence and the main types of inference and judgment, and, with regard to each of these, to explain its nature and special merits and defects."[3]

2. JUDGMENT AND IDEA

I. Bradley's treatment of idea, judgment, and inference is an analogue of his conclusions concerning them, in that the consideration of each is qualified by constant reference to the others. His interest in them is an interest in the forms of thought by which it has been said that we can attain truth; it is not an interest in elements and operations in a system of formal relations. His very choice of words helps to substantiate such an interpretation; the word, "implication," as a logical term, does not appear once in the body of *The Principles of Logic,* (so crowded with considerations of "inference") and makes its appearance for the first time in the *Terminal Essays,* where it occupies a subordinate position.[4] This does not, of course, involve Bradley in what he deplores as the "psychological attitude," the habit of thinking of the terms of judgment as some kind of mental existences.

---

[3] *PL,* p. 620.

[4] Bradley's interest throughout is not only in inference rather than implication but in judgment rather than proposition. Indeed the word "proposition" is not even listed in the index.

It is by means of an attack on this attitude, indeed, that he introduces the subject of the nature of ideas.

II. That ideas are mental existences, states, images, etc. Bradley does not deny; what he refuses to allow is that it is the idea as existence that functions in judgment. Like all other existences, ideas are both content and existence—the familiar "what" and "that" of *Appearance and Reality*. But they are only ideas if they possess a third quality, that of signifying something other than themselves. And it is alone as signification or meaning that they function for logic. "We might say that, in the end, there are no signs save ideas, but what I here wish to insist on is that, for logic at least, all ideas are signs."[5] In actual judgment there is always a mental state corresponding to the idea predicated but "it is clear that the idea, which we use as the predicate of the judgment, is not my mental state as such."[6] If I predicate B of A, I do not mean that A is actually qualified by my mental image of B, but by B itself. "The idea in judgment is the universal meaning; it is not ever the occasional imagery, and still less can it be the whole psychical event."[7]

III. As an introduction to the subject the above is a simple and clear statement of the meaning of idea for logic. The full meaning must wait on an introductory exposition of the nature of judgment and of inference, as each of those must wait on the other. The development of Bradley's theory of judgment, however, got off to what he later (in the notes and *Terminal Essays* in the *Logic,* as well as in other places) considered a false start. One of the presuppositions with which he started, based perhaps on the notion of idea as sign, was the doctrine of "floating ideas," a belief that ideas in themselves did not qualify reality but were merely "wandering adjectives."[8] One of the consequences of this assumption which caused Bradley much concern but which, typically, he none the less accepted, was the doctrine that negative judgments do not as such hold of reality. The way in which this follows from a belief in "floating ideas" is more evident if we examine the expression of that belief in his early statements about truth. "By the truth of a judgment," he writes, "we mean that its suggestion is more than an idea, that it is fact or in fact."[9] The falsehood of a judgment would mean, then, that its suggestion is *merely* an idea, that it is not fact or in fact.

---

[5] *PL,* p. 5.
[6] *PL,* p. 8.
[7] *PL,* p. 10.
[8] The meaning of "floating ideas" is elaborated in Chapter VI, section 2.
[9] *PL,* p. 10.

There are grave difficulties in the way of developing this doctrine. A "floating idea" can never be the thing it means or intends, for otherwise error could not be explained. But in a true judgment we have more than an abstract meaning; we actually have fact. If an idea were to be regarded as some kind of mental counter, although not merely a mental existence, by what alchemy could this abstraction be transmuted into fact, fact being taken to mean, presumably, that which the idea signifies? Of course it could be said that in a true judgment the idea represented, or corresponded to, the fact, but that is not what Bradley means. The difficulty, impossibility perhaps, of developing this doctrine consistently comes from the use of "idea" in such a way that it implies a correspondence theory of truth, while "truth" is at the same time taken to mean some sort of identity of the idea with the object it signifies. The use of three theories of truth throughout the first edition of *The Principles of Logic* resulted, as I shall try to show, in a confusion which was later dispelled by distinguishing three realms, each with its own criterion of truth, only one of which, however, was regarded as ultimately valid.

A negative judgment, of course, is equivalent to the denial of the truth of its contradictory, which is an affirmative judgment, and so partakes of the unreal character of falsehood. "It (the negative judgment) asserts that a predicate is incompatible, but it does not say that either the predicate or the incompatibility are real facts."[10] There is, however, no implication here that negation or denial is completely apart from reality in its consequences, only the notion that the idea that is denied has no being, save as psychical existence, perhaps, and is for logic merely a "wandering adjective". Its connection with reality is based on Bradley's doctrine that all denial implies a ground. "Denial or contradiction is not the same thing as the assertion of the contrary; but in the end it can rest on nothing else."[11] This is not equivalent to asserting that the contradictory of what is denied must itself be fact—the particular subject of the judgment may not even exist. "Logical negation always contradicts, but never asserts the existence of the contradictory. To say "A is not B" is merely the same as to deny that "A is B", or to assert that "A is B" is false. And since it can not go beyond this result, a mere denial of B can never assert that the contradictory Not-B is real. The fact it does assert is the existence of an opposite incompatible quality, either in the immediate or ultimate subject."[12] To deny that Socrates is well is not to assert

---
[10] *PL*, p. 121.
[11] *PL*, p. 123.
[12] *PL*, p. 122.

that he is ill, for Socrates has long since passed beyond either health or illness.

With the elimination some time later, of the doctrine of "floating ideas", Bradley was constrained to revise his account of judgment in the direction of other tendencies in his original account, emphasis falling at times on factors which he had failed to stress; in addition, it became necessary to purge the *Logic* of the consequences of what he regarded as an erroneous belief.

IV. Bradley's early definition of judgment, on which the second edition of the *Logic* contains a long critical note, is stated thus: "Judgment proper is the act which refers an ideal content (recognized as such) to a reality beyond the act."[13] The reference of the idea to reality is twofold,[14] the subject proper being a particular content which, if the judgment is true, is contained in Reality, and the ultimate subject being Reality itself which, we affirm, must have such a character that the judgment can be true. ". . . judgment is the act which, while it recognizes the idea as appearance, nevertheless goes on to predicate it. It either attributes the idea to reality, and so affirms that the idea is true, or pronounces it to be merely a bare idea, and that the facts exclude the meaning it suggests. The ideal content which is also fact, and the ideal content which is nothing beyond itself, are truth and falsehood as they appear in judgment."[15]

The notion that in judgment we are confronted with two ideas Bradley stigmatizes as the grossest of errors. The mere fact that most judgments contain a subject and a predicate is certainly insufficient evidence for concluding that each signifies a separate idea. "This apple is red" conveys, not an idea of apple and an idea of redness, but the single idea of a red apple. Ultimately the form of the judgment, which attributes something to reality, may be rendered thus: "Reality is such that this apple is red." Only one idea is contained in the judgment and that idea is either affirmed or denied of reality.

V. The notion that judgment contains but one idea may lead the reader to a postscript of his own on the nature of ideas in such a context. If each term in a judgment were a sign standing for an idea, the terms might very well have their meanings fixed apart from the judgment itself; and any assertion or denial would be concerned with the

---

[13] *PL*, p. 10.

[14] The twofold aspect of the subject is a theme emphasized and developed in the *Terminal Essays*.

[15] *PL*, p. 33. This definition, of course, contains the notion of "floating ideas." It is interesting to note Bradley's continuous use of the word "act" in writing of judgment, a fact on which he himself comments (PL, p. 39, n. 10), in connection with the interest he exhibits throughout in thinking as a function.

relation, in some respect, of ideas to each other, not with the meaning of each idea. If, on the other hand, the entire judgment predicates of reality, or denies to it, one idea, then the meaning of that idea resides in the judgment. Meaning, as a whole, must be thought of as fluid, the terms tentatively suggesting some meaning and judgments containing those terms clarifying the meaning and making it more precise. Ultimately, the full meaning of any sign would be found in the sum total of true judgments and so would be something beyond mortal attainment. This doctrine follows from what has gone before because the clarification of the meaning of any sign could be brought about, not by any one judgment containing that sign (unless it were, perhaps, a single proposition summarizing all truth), but by the totality of all true judgments in which that sign is a term. There remains, however, the relation of the meaning so far established, to the rest of reality, a relation which is fully explained only by all other true judgments.

If we substitute, in the above account, the term "truth" for the term "meaning", we shall have another of the consequences of the doctrine that each judgment contains but one idea. For if each judgment contained a statement of some relation between two or more ideas, we might conclude that the truth or falsehood of that judgment could be ascertained without reference, for it would be irrelevant, to a totality of true judgments. The meaning of the terms once stated, there would be only a question of whether the relation in the judgment did or did not actually hold. If the judgment contains only the one idea, however, then it is meaningful to predicate truth or falsehood of ideas. And the truth of an idea is in the same case as its meaning; one cannot very well hold that an idea is absolutely true if he does not know what it means. A term cannot be completely true, for its meaning is subject to constant modification in a series of judgments. But the meaning of any idea, it seems, is only partially delineated in any judgment. Its truth, then, in any one judgment, is as partial as its meaning; complete truth, like full meaning, is to be found only in the totality of true judgments.

Any thinker who starts along the lines of this argument will find it difficult to avoid being committed to some doctrine of degrees of truth and falsehood. Bradley, though he revised much of the early part of his book by the time he came to the end of the *Terminal Essays,* nevertheless clung to sufficient of the essentials of this position so that, even were there no other theoretical seeds in his logic which would flower in a theory of degrees of truth, he had such a doctrine already implicit in his argument.

3. MODALITY

I. The negative judgment provided an obstacle in the path of the attempt to interpret all assertion and denial as referring ultimately to Reality itself, an obstacle which Bradley was to eliminate with some care.[16] Yet it was but one of several types of judgment which it was important to exhibit as conformable to this general interpretation. Compound judgments fit easily into the pattern, for they are composed of categoricals. The hypothetical, for instance, asserts that something is the case subject to a condition. And that condition must itself be grounded in Reality in order for the consequent to be affirmed as a true categorical. Forms which called on Bradley for an exercise of the ingenuity he displayed in the treatment of negation are those which traditionally have been called "modal." It is important to divagate for a moment from the development of our central theme in order to show how modality fits into Bradley's scheme. Later, negation will be considered in the same way.

II. The welding of all possible logical forms into a system which exhibited all thought as containing a dependence on, and an ultimate reference to, Reality, was essential to the consistent exposition of Bradley's logical beliefs. Every step taken towards that end was a step towards the development of a sceptical weapon which could be used to give the quietus to much traditional metaphysics. It is the contention of this essay that to understand all judgment as an ascription of some character to Reality constitutes an acceptance of scepticism. The refusal to discriminate specific contexts within which specific judgments hold, their truth being irrelevant to other contexts, involves an attempt to construct a vast system of the whole within which truth would be completeness and completeness would be impossible. On the basis of conclusions derived from the consideration of the nature of such a system, rival metaphysicians could be discomfited and many of the accepted categories of philosophy could be destroyed. Thus every advance in the development of such a system, every new application of Bradley's analysis of the judgment, can be regarded as a sharpening of the sceptical weapon which he was later to wield so effectively. The treatment of modality can be understood from this point of view as one of the processes in the course of which Bradley's instrument was forged. I shall limit myself, therefore, to that in Bradley's treatment which is relevant to these considerations and shall forego much, however provocative and stimulating, of his discussion.

III. Modality is, traditionally, logical qualification of a meaningful

---

[16] See next chapter, section 3.

utterance in terms of the modes possibile, impossibile, contingens, necessarium. Bradley's treatment of the impossible is subordinate to his treatment of the other forms and, indeed, impossibility is not specifically mentioned as one of the modal forms. Of these, he thinks, there are three basic types: the possible, the necessary, and the actual, or real. The innumerable forms of psychological qualification (I wish, I hope, etc.) are swept aside as not being pertinent to his theme. "I wish S—P were true," for example, is not a logical mode of S—P, for neither S—P nor any qualification of it is asserted as true or false.

Little attention need be paid the assertorical mode, that which asserts actuality, for it may be identified with the categorical judgment. The latter always has reference to Reality, always asserts that its content is real. The assertorical mode, therefore, is no special qualification of a categorical judgment but is the categorical judgment itself. Although Bradley does not make the point, what he is doing throughout the *Logic* constitutes an attempt to show that all types of judgment are forms of the assertorical, or, at least, dependent upon it.

IV. The qualification of a judgment in the ways expressed by the modes possible and necessary, Bradley argues, have to do, respectively, with what may be and what must be. Thus it may be seen that they depend upon a condition and so may be treated as forms of the hypothetical. "A necessary truth may be, and commonly is, categorical, but, so far as its necessity goes, it is hypothetical."[17] Here the question arises: what, if the assertoric, and thus the categorical, are to be regarded as contingent, is the domain of the necessary? Bradley's answer is that the only kind of necessity is logical necessity, that is, the necessity by which certain evidence will yield a certain conclusion. In other language, we might say that the only necessity is that of implication, the necessity, for example, with which q follows if we are given the conjunctive "p implies q, and p." Bradley's own statement is: "For logic what is necessary is nothing beyond a logical consequence. Necessity is here the force which compels us to go to a conclusion, if we start from premises."[18] And, as to a counterpart in Reality: "The bond of necessity is a logical passage, and to say that this logical passage itself exists in fact demands an assumption which can not be hazarded in the face of objections."[18]

Since I do not wish, in the future chapters of this essay, to revive the discussion of modality in terms of Bradley's later approach as found, for instance, in the *Terminal Essays*, I think it is proper, at this point, to quote one of the notes appended by Bradley in revision

[17] *PL*, p. 200.
[18] *PL*, p. 201.

of this discussion. " . . . logic most certainly should not admit and assume that its 'because' is not real. To regard logical implication as merely 'ideal' is an error."[19] The statement is a consequence of Bradley's shift from belief in "floating ideas" to the doctrine that all ideas qualify reality. The precise meaning of that doctrine and of this note will be considered hereafter. Suffice it to say that because of this change in belief Bradley's treatment of the possible and the necessary as, somehow, subjective, would have to undergo appropriate revision.

The necessary being regarded here as simply a logical bond it may even be the case that "the necessary may be impossible or non-existent."[20] As an example of necessary connection in which the elements connected are neither existent nor possible, Bradley offers the judgment: "If two were three, then four must be six."[21]

Both the necessary and the possible are to be regarded as hypothetical, and the possible as a form of the necessary. "The possible," Bradley writes, "is that which is known or assumed to be the consequence of certain conditions. So far the possible is one with the necessary, where it is implied that the antecedent is real. But it differs in this point; for S-P to be possible all the conditions which make S-P necessary must be supposed, but only a part of them need be assumed to exist. It is assumed that a part of the antecedent exists, but as to the other part we are left in ignorance. Thus the *partial* existence of the conditions of S-P is the *differentia* which separates the species 'possible' from the genus 'necessary.' "[22]

Since knowledge of the conditions upon which any possibility is dependent may be anything from very slight to thorough, the varieties of possibility are enormous. At its highest, possibility depends upon conditions which are completely known, but only a portion of which are taken as existing; at its lowest, possibility is merely that which is "not known to be impossible."[23]

V. The impossible is nothing at all if it is regarded as the self-contradictory, for then it is meaningless. If it is not a contradiction, then it is something which the universe cannot support. "The impossible is that which must be unreal. We might call it, if we chose, one kind of the necessary."[24] Although the impossible is not itself a contradiction, it is dependent upon contradiction. The conditions under which alone

---

[19] *PL*, p. 236, note 6.
[20] *PL*, p. 202.
[21] *PL*, p. 201.
[22] *PL*, p. 202f.
[23] *PL*, p. 203.
[24] *PL*, p. 213.

something can exist may be incompatible with conditions known to exist. If this is the case the thing under consideration is impossible.

The necessary, it has been said before, is only a logical bond. Therefore to call the impossible a form of the necessary must be to mean that its impossibility is a logical impossibility. This, I think, implies an appeal to some theory of truth as coherence, for the distinguishing characteristic of the impossible is its failure to be coherent with the system of judgments which constitutes knowledge. Bradley's language may seem to be about existence rather than discourse, but one must remember that, in all his writing, he assumes discourse to contain a constant reference to the real, so that statements about the one are usually translatable into statements about the other. The way in which Bradley states the above point about the impossible in terms of Reality, is as follows: "The impossible we see must imply a positive quality, known or assumed to belong to the real. If X is impossible this means and must mean that an actual X would remove by its presence some positive attribute we take to be real."[25]

VI. Our conclusions as to Bradley's treatment of modality may be summarized: (1) The assertorical is not really a modal form since it does not qualify a judgment in any way, being indeed the type of the categorical judgment; (2) the possible and, in a sense, the impossible, are forms of the necessary; (3) the necessary and its forms are hypothetical in that they depend upon a condition or conditions, having a basis in fact, or, in other language, depending upon one or more categorical judgments; (4) the possible is differentiated within the class "necessary" in that only a part of its conditions are assumed to exist; (5) the impossible is differentiated within the class "necessary" in that its conditions are incompatible with what is known to be real; (6) the necessary itself is that which must follow on the basis of certain conditions.

All modal forms have thus been shown to be dependent upon Reality as are the ordinary forms of judgment. This has been done by showing that modal forms are either indistinguishable from, or ultimately dependent on, the categorical judgment. "We have shown that the necessary as well as the possible has a basis in fact and depends upon experience. A modal judgment has to make an assertion about reality."[26] Thus the analysis of the judgment with which Bradley started his logical studies is further justified by the breadth of its scope, and is made more secure as a sceptical principle.

---
[25] *PL*, p. 213.
[26] *PL*, p. 209.

4. INFERENCE

I. That thought, for Bradley, is an organic whole is not only suggested by the way in which idea and judgment are interwoven so that they are aspects of the same thing, judgment being a kind of fulfillment of idea, but it is borne out by the manner in which they both dovetail into inference.

"An inference is either a result or a process. If we take it as a result, we saw that it is the apprehension of a necessary truth. If we take it as a process, it is simply the operation which leads to that result. A truth judged true because of something else, and the going to a truth from the ground of a judgment or supposition are what we mean by conclusion and reasoning."[27] Anxious to utilize every opportunity to lay the ghost of "floating ideas," Bradley adds a note: "But to take 'supposition' as excluding 'judgment' is wrong. There are no 'mere ideas.' "[28]

Inference has three characteristic features.[29] First, inference is not the same as observation. To perceive a thing, no matter how closely, is not to have an inference, for an inference depends on a basis already established. Second, an inference is never an isolated unit. It proceeds from its basis and is the result of a process (in conformity with the extended quotation above we should add, "or the process itself.") Third, an inference must contain some information, and that information must be something other than the information contained in the judgments upon which it rests. "An inference must be more than a vain repetition, and its result is no echo of senseless iteration."[30]

The third of these characteristics might lead the reader to suppose that the result of an inference is never to be regarded as analytic of the judgments on which it is based, but Bradley's explication of the point in the *Terminal Essays* shows that this is not what he meant—or, at any rate, it is not what he meant in his later considerations. This contention, in any event, sets the stage for what he calls "the essential puzzle of inference."[31]

As a statement of the structure of inference, Bradley writes: "Every inference contains two elements: it is in the first place a process, and in the second place a result. The process is an operation of synthesis; it takes its *data* and by ideal construction combines them

---
[27] *PL*, p. 243.
[28] *PL*, p. 244.
[29] *PL*, p. 245.
[30] *PL*, p. 245.
[31] *PL*, p. 599.

into a whole. The result is the perception of a new relation within that unity. We start with certain relations of elements; by virtue of the sameness of two or more of these elements we unite their relations in one single construction, and in that we perceive a fresh unity of these elements. What is given to us is terms conjoined; we operate on these conjunctions and put them together into a (connected[32]) whole; and the conclusion is the perception of two terms in relation, which were not (so[32]) related before the operation. Thus the process is a construction and the result an intuition, while the union of both is logical demonstration."[33]

This notion of a new relation in the conclusion of the inference, the information referred to before, which is not contained in the evidence, raises for Bradley a problem to which he recurs more than once. Towards the end of the second volume he states his difficulty in more detail than at his first consideration of inference. It is perhaps the case, he argues,[34] that the conclusion contains nothing that is not in the premises. If so, it cannot be a real conclusion, in any legitimate sense of the word. The information is there already and we have not gone any farther than our starting point. If, on the other hand, we have proceeded beyond what we started with, where did the additional information come from? If outside the premises, then the evidence which yields the information should have been included within them. And we would be in the same case as in our first supposition. But there is another possibility: the conclusion may be new and may follow from the premises because we made it that way. Conclusions are arrived at by mental operations and it may well be that these operations are responsible for the conclusion being what it is. The conclusion of our dilemma is, then, that either the conclusions of our inferences are mere echoes, a mumbled repetition of what we already have, or they follow from our premises only with a condition, namely, that we think them so.

II. There are many to whom one of Bradley's auctorial virtues is not his avoidance of mere verbal problems, and the argument above might seem a case in point. Certainly we have here an instance of much ado about nothing which a few simple distinctions, like that between logical and psychological novelty, might eliminate, unless Bradley is confronted with some difficulty more fundamental to his argument which the solution to his dilemma serves to reveal. That there is

---

[32] Inserted in a note as one of the author's revisions.
[33] *PL*, p. 256.
[34] *PL*, pp. 552-4.

such a difficulty his discussion of the same dilemmatic situation in the *Terminal Essays* makes more emphatic.

When he broaches his problem in the body of the book he manages to escape, with no danger of having his argument impaled, between the horns. "We must meet the dilemma by a saving distinction. We have here nothing to do with the *real* validity of our reasoning process, but solely with its soundness as a logical transition. And hence at present we need to regard our reasoning as simply a change in our way of knowing. But this breaks through the circle which threatened to be fatal; for it shows a possibility which was overlooked. If, by altering *myself* I so am able to perceive a connection which before was not visible, then my act conditions, not the consequence itself, but my knowledge of that consequence. It goes to make the consequence in my recognition, but stands wholly apart from the truth which I recognize. Though the function of concluding depends upon my intellect, the content concluded may be wholly unhelped, untouched, and self-developed."[35] The distinction between logical and psychological novelty seems indeed the solution to the puzzle but the last sentence quoted has not in any way been justified by such a distinction. If our reasoning is "simply a change in our way of knowing," then the development in information from premises to conclusion is something that would not exist for omniscience. It is a function of a limited intelligence. What, then, does it mean to say that "the content concluded may be wholly unhelped, untouched, and self-developed?" If it is unhelped in that we do not in any sense "make" the conclusion but simply apprehend it, then it is obvious that the conclusion was already there (and "there" can only mean "in the premises") to be apprehended. In this case it is difficult to see in what sense the content concluded may be said to be self-developed. And if the words "unhelped" and "untouched" have any other meaning, I fail to understand what it can be.

That Bradley was aware of difficulties in resolving this problem of inference in the manner stated above can readily be seen in a number of the notes which appear at the end of chapters in the revised edition, notes which apprehend a fresh bout with the issue in the *Terminal Essays*. Before considering the manner in which he restates his position in that place, it might be valuable to append one of his notes in revision. Having, in the text, written: "new truth, that is truth new *to us*,"[36] he comments, at the end of the chapter: "We have here a serious error. The question, as to novelty *to me*, is wholly irrelevant.

---
[35] *PL*, p. 554f.
[36] *PL*, p. 406.

The real question is as to whether the subject developes itself ideally into something different or not."[37] In order to understand this comment it is, of course, of vital importance to know what Bradley means by "the subject." On that meaning, indeed, depends any answer to the question as to whether the importance assigned to the whole problem by Bradley is due to its being regarded by him as a knotty problem in logic or, rather, as basic to the pursuit of metaphysical truth. We must, however, postpone further discussion until our consideration of the *Terminal Essays*.

5. JUDGMENT AND INFERENCE

I. Though elements in a whole can be treated separately, to some extent, a full understanding of them must wait on a study of their relations to each other and, ultimately, on some description of the whole. This is an old ideal in philosophy, this "seeing things clearly and seeing them whole." Carried to its logical conclusions it implies a monistic universe (whose essence, every ambitious monist hopes, can be summed up in the language of a single principle), or else it is the expression of an ideal limit for discourse ("whose margin fades forever and forever" as we approach it). If we are to accept, in any of its possible meanings, this ancient aspiration for one of our own, we are committed, at least, to some belief in system, be it in existence or in discourse.

System was a fundamental principle to Bradley; system in both discourse and existence. In *The Principles of Logic* he attempted to exhibit the system that was discourse; in *Appearance and Reality* the system that was existence. And the analogies between the two are striking, as they must be, for Bradley ultimately treated them as aspects of the same thing.

II. The manner in which idea and judgment can be considered, to a certain extent, one, has already been exhibited. There remains the necessity of performing the same service for judgment and inference. To exhibit to what extent two things can be said to be different and to what extent the same, was for Bradley a kind of pleasurable compulsion, for in that manner it was possible to give instance after instance of the "diversity in unity" which was so favorite a theme of his.

---

[37] *PL*, p. 425, note 15. On this subject see also p. 403. "The process . . . to my vision," and in comment, p. 424, note 11. In the latter citation, he makes the interesting statement: "It is wrong (I should now say) to call any process an inference if it fails both to *show* and also to *be* the self-development of a real object."

Both judgment and inference, insofar as they are merely rudimentary and have not yet become explicit, constitute a nexus of such a character that a link of one precedes a link of the other and is itself proceeded by a link of the first, ad infinitum or, at any rate, as far back as we can go. When they become explicit, judgment is to be distinguished from inference chiefly on the ground that the former, in any single inferential process, stands in no need of evidence to support it; while the latter is, in essence, an operation proceeding from evidence as a base. On the other hand, every inference culminates in a judgment and that in turn may become a premise for further inferences, and so on. In this sense they are parts of one process. " . . . explicit judgment and inference, acts both of which end in an asserted truth, and one of which starts with a truth laid down as the foundation of its process. And *in this sense* it is true that we judge before we reason, since we become possessed of an affirmation, when we cannot produce any other affirmation on which this stands. Thus the distinction which we made remains unshaken. Explicit judgment comes before explicit inference. And supposing that both are really and in the end two sides of one act, then the above conclusion is what we might have expected. Here as everywhere the product comes to consciousness first, and the process afterwards."[38]

III. The notion that judgment and inference "are really and in the end two sides of one act," has direct bearing on the theory of meaning which we discussed in connection with the relation of idea to judgment. The terms of any judgment, we saw, contribute to the meaning of the single idea expressed by that judgment. The idea itself, which is partially clarified by the individual judgment and whose ultimate meaning resides in the totality of true judgments, is rendered somewhat more explicit by any valid inference within which it functions as a judgment. Such an inference by its very nature exhibits the connection between that idea and some other idea to which it is related (the relation already existing between the two being, of course, the middle term). To state the matter in another way: an idea, one aspect of which is expressed in a judgment, and a second aspect of which is expressed in another judgment, is stated more completely in the conclusion of an inference which uses both judgments as premises.

Inference may, perhaps, be regarded in still another manner as being essential to the growth of meaning. The totality of true judgments which are necessary for the completion of any meaning must constitute a system; for if they do not, meanings could not be adequately

---

[38] *PL*, p. 481.

exhibited. There would be no growth of meaning, no final expression of essence, unless the entire judgmental complex constituted one system in which the idea was exhibited ever more clearly until it reached completion. System itself has no intelligible meaning unless the parts are related to each other and every part to the whole. And the kind of relation that holds throughout? This being the system of discourse, the relation must be logical, it must be such that the mind can travel from a part to the whole; in short, the relation must be inferential. It is on inference, then, as the very essence of the totality of true judgments, that meaning depends, for without inference one could not even proceed from the individual judgment which partially expresses one idea to the other judgments which are necessary to the development of its meaning.

6 JUDGMENT, INFERENCE, AND TRUTH

I. The relation between the structure of discourse and the structure of reality, a theme on which Bradley played many variations, was, in his opinion, a problem whose solution would confer on some of our judgments the accolade of truth or, perhaps, relegate all possible judgments to the limbo of falsehood. The question of "the validity of inference," by which he means the question as to whether inference is a process capable of attaining truth, is of course at one with the question as to whether any judgment can be true, unless there are ways of formulating true judgments apart from inference: by intuition, perhaps, or revelation. If one were to maintain this latter position, and to deny that any inference can culminate in a truth, he would be confronted with the necessity of maintaining also that a true judgment could have no consequences in discourse, since those consequences would be the result of some form of inference. But should he accept this he would be in the position of accepting an implication, the validity of which he denies, of his own belief. And should he deny it, as he would deny all judgments based on inference, he would be outside the realm of communication.

No such notion, certainly, is propounded here by Bradley. A treatise on logic, in any event, would seem the last place where one would expect to encounter such a doctrine. Bradley is using the age-old technique of the real sceptic; he is discounting all other avenues to truth save reason (which, though it need not be taken as identical with logic, certainly includes it) and then proceeding to demonstrate that reason cannot yield truth. And if it be objected that the very use of the word "demonstrate" implies that he must use reason in his attack on reason and so defeat his aim, it can be answered that if reason can be shown to be inadequate in terms of its own criteria, it has been struck a death blow and awaits not even a coup de grace. This is in a sense the technique of Hume and even of Kant who, though they later introduce other notions, write a good many sentences to show that, in its own terms and without the adoption of any contra-logical principles, reason is not capable of yielding truth, save, perhaps, in a limited sense. And when one strikes at the rational processes by attacking logic itself he is not attempting to turn a flank but is trying to crumble the center.

II. In order to show how the possibility of attaining truth dissolves on Bradley's treatment of judgment and inference, it is important to consider the manner in which he reduces all categorical judgment to the form of the hypothetical. It has already been said that throughout the *Logic* Bradley was concerned with exhibiting the dependence of all types of judgment on the categorical.[39] Here I shall attempt to clarify the sense in which this is so. I shall consider first Bradley's analysis of the universal judgment and then his analysis of the particular and the singular, following these with a note on disjunction.

The universal judgment is easily interpreted as having the meaning of a hypothetical. "The fact that is asserted in an abstract judgment is not the existence of the subject or predicate, but simply the connection between the two. And this connection rests on a supposal. The abstract universal, 'A is B,' means no more than 'given A, in that case B,' or 'if A, then B.' In short such judgments are always hypothetical and can never be categorical."[40]

In considering other types of categorical judgment, the particular may be regarded as included in the treatment of what Bradley calls singular judgments. Of these he distinguishes three types. "(i) We have first those judgments which make an assertion about that which I now perceive, or feel, or about some portion of it. 'I have a toothache,' 'There is a wolf,' 'That bough is broken.' In these we simply analyze the given, and may therefore call them by the name of *Analytic judgments of sense*. Then (ii) we have *Synthetic judgments of sense*, which state either some fact of time or space, or again some quality of the matter given, which I do not here and now directly perceive. 'This road leads to London,' 'Yesterday it rained,' 'Tomorrow there will be a full moon.' They are synthetic because they extend the given through an ideal construction, and they all, as we shall see, involve an inference. The third class (iii), on the other hand, have to do with a reality which is never a sensible event in time. 'God is a

---

[39] See the discussion of Modality, Chapter 2, section 3.
[40] *PL*, p. 82.

spirit,' 'The soul is a substance.' We may think what we like of the validity of these judgments, and may or may not decline to recognize them in metaphysics. But in logic they certainly must have a place."[41]

These singular judgments are dependent for their truth on the Whole from which they are abstracted; at any moment they are elements within some larger context and their truth is dependent upon the character of that context. To put it otherwise, these judgments are true only if a whole series of conditions upon which they depend are true. So they may be regarded as hypothetical and any assertion of them implies as antecedent: "If certain conditions are true." Bradley's treatment of the analytic judgment (the terminology, of course, has a different meaning from that employed by Kant) is typical of what can be said of the other kinds. "The analytic judgment is not true *per se*. It can not stand by itself. Asserting, as it does, of the particular presentation, it must always suppose a further content, which falls outside that fraction it affirms. What it says is true, if true at all, because of something else. The fact it states is really fact only in relation to the rest of the context, and only because of the rest of that context. It is not true except under that condition."[42]

All categorical judgments are hypothetical. But the antecedents in such hypothetical judgments are ultimately categoricals. Since these, like all other categoricals, are essentially hypothetical, it seems that an endless series is involved. And, I suppose, this is actually the case. Yet in a completed system of knowledge the hypothetical character of judgments would disappear, for we would no longer say: "If this, then that," but rather: "This, therefore that."[43]

The disjunctive judgment, to dispose, for our purposes, of a very interesting topic, in a brief note, partakes of the character of the hypothetical and so, ultimately, of the categorical. To say "A is b or c" is to combine four hypothetical judgments: "If A is b, it is not c;" "If A is c, it is not b;" "If A is not b, it is c;" and "If A is not c, it is b." Bradley considers disjunction as containing elements of the hypothetical and elements of the categorical. " . . . the essence of disjunctive judgment is not got by calling it a combination of supposals. It has a distinctive character of its own. It first takes a predicate known within limits, and defined by exclusion, and then further

---

[41] *PL*, p. 82.
[42] *PL*, p. 97f.
[43] On the other hand, it is essential to emphasize that, insofar as we do not have a completed system, all categorical judgments are hypothetical. Bradley regards this as strong evidence for an ultimate scepticism.

defines it by hypothetical exclusion. It rests on the assumption that we have the whole field, and by removing parts can determine the residue. It supposes in short a kind of omniscience. Its assertion again, if not quite categorical, is certainly not quite hypothetical. It involves both these elements."[44]

III. Bradley's way of showing that inference cannot yield truth, depends ultimately on the contention that discourse and reality are diverse in structure. There are, he insists, but three alternatives. "Our actual process may be foreign to reality, and falls outside it in our mental world. Or an actual and answering change has taken place, and the facts are transformed by our caprice. Or lastly the course of things run parallel by an overruling harmony. Any one of these alternatives seems attended with ruin."[45]

Let us consider the last two first. If the facts are altered by what we think them to be, then the distinctions of truth and falsehood which we usually make are completely meaningless; more confusing still, if a number of people believe incompatible things about the universe at the same time, all those things must at that time be facts in the universe.

On the notion that there is a harmony of such a nature that existence parallels discourse we are forced to "suppose that each trivial argument, every wretched illustration that we may have used in these discussions, provided only it be free from flaw, must have its direct counterpart in the nature of things."[46] This is very much the same as the first alternative for, unless we believe that our thinking has some divine guidance (and we cannot, since we constantly encounter contradiction), we must accept the belief that the world is somehow harmonized with whatever we happen to think (and we cannot, since the world would have to contain our every contradiction). If there be a Mind that shapes thought and existence into a harmony, that Mind would be guilty of the very inconsistencies which we refuse to accept. Here it is necessary to include a word of criticism. This alternative is capable of being formulated in two different ways, quite divergent in their meanings. Bradley's ability to destroy this second possibility (like his ability to use the method of elimination here and so arrive at the necessity of accepting his third alternative) is due to the simple error of not exhausting the alternatives. The doctrine of harmony need not be taken to mean that all thinking, of whatever character, must be a counterpart of existential structure;

---

[44] *PL*, p. 137.
[45] *PL*, p. 581.
[46] *PL*, p. 582.

it might mean that some thinking harmonizes with the world in being a description of some part of it. Refusal to think of the notion of "harmony" after this fashion makes Bradley's conclusions the destruction of cardboard soldiers. And, of course, there are a number of other unconsidered alternatives among which, perhaps, lies the true one.

The third alternative, which we must accept on this view, is that some reasoning is not in conformity with nature. Nor do I think that any one would hesitate in offering his agreement. But Bradley quickly goes farther. No reasoning can represent nature. "We shall have to see that our mental experiment can *never* represent the actual event. And our conclusions also are threatened with falsehood; for our arguments can not even finish with a truth. Both process and result diverge from given reality. They no doubt may be valid in the sense of serving, they may go near enough to convey the meaning,[47] but neither can be called correct translations.

"If the result seems strange, it is strange because we have not remembered our account of judgment. It is in a judgment that our reasoning must end; and our natural impulse is to think that ideas are divided and joined like the things which we know. But we saw that this notion could not be verified. Our hypothetical, disjunctive, and negative judgments were none of them found to represent facts. There is nothing left which, if truth is a copy, could possibly be true, save only the class of categoric judgments. And, seeking for these, we failed wholly to find them, so long as we kept to the series of phenomena. All our ordinary truths, every single affirmation we were able to make about the course of events, turned out in the end to be hypothetical. We tried in vain to get right down to the facts; we were always left with an artificial extract and a fragment got by mutilating things. And this product failed of truth in two ways. It left out details which it ought to have copied, and it depended on details which did not exist. However you took it, it turned out hypothetical, and the elements which it connected lacked actual existence.

"And this failure was a symptom of our logical disease, a weakness not passing, nor local in its area, but deep-rooted in the system. For judgment and inference, if we are to have them at all, must both be *discursive;* they must work with ideas. But ideas (as such)[48] do not exist, and they can not exist, if existence means presence in the series of phenomena . . . the idea is a content, which, being

---

[47] Only a tentative, or "practical" meaning, in accordance with the implications we have drawn from Bradley's doctrines.

[48] Inserted in a correction, p. 594, note 16.

universal, is no phenomenon. The image in my head exists psychologically, and outside it the fact has particular existence, for they both are events. But the idea (as such[48]) does not happen and it can not possess a place in the series. It is a mutilated content which, as such, can not claim to be more than an adjective. And the functions, that work with these unrealities, can not possibly reproduce the flow of events."[49]

IV. I have quoted the above passages at some length because they contain Bradley's final opinions (in the body of the book) on the status of judgment and inference with regard to truth. A number of comments must be made. Even if we grant that ideas are meanings and not existences, and that the use of ideas is the essential characteristic of discourse, it is difficult to see why they should be referred to as "these unrealities," except, perhaps, insofar as they are "wandering adjectives," or why it should follow that the use of them "can not possibly reproduce the flow of events." Bradley is writing on the assumption that, in some sense, "truth is a copy," but despite his many warnings that we cannot expect the judgmental complex to *be* the existence it seeks to reveal, he seems to be denying that discourse can reproduce existence because it is not identical with it. An admonition is doubly wasted if its own author forgets it.

As to the use of the "copy" theory of truth, it should be noted that Bradley writes, in his revision: "The attempt made at times in this work for the sake of convenience to identify reality with the series of facts, and truth with copying—was, I think, misjudged."[50] If the attempt was made merely "for the sake of convenience" it was, indeed, unfortunate. The force of any argument concerning the power of human reason to attain truth rests upon the definition of truth involved. It is quite absurd to show that discourse cannot attain a copy of existence and then to urge that, although such a copy may not be what one means by truth, this constitutes evidence to prove that discourse is forever condemned to the darkness of error or of illusion. Yet this is just what Bradley, at times, seems to be doing.

Side by side with the constant references to truth as a copy are the statements concerning idea, judgment and inference—the basis of the work—yielding the clear implication that truth should be defined as some form of coherence. Truth, on Bradley's fundamental principles, must be bound up with the type of development which, I have tried to show, meaning must have in such a system. Perhaps it is a function of Bradley's willingness to inject metaphysical

---

[49] *PL*, p. 583f.
[50] *PL*, p. 591, note 1.

problems into his logic and his refusal to give metaphysical conclusions—at any length—but he develops a system of logical theory whose implications remain unexpressed while he utters doctrines actually inconsistent with what follows from his chief theses.

This inconsistency did not remain hidden from Bradley's eyes and, of course, he was at great pains to correct it, but for our purposes it is important to note that it was there. Those who try to blame Bradley for his philosophical vices often overlook the careful corrections he made of all his work, whereas those whose purpose it is to commend him for his virtues show a tendency to neglect, or at least to minimize, his first utterances on any subject, while emphasizing the acuteness of his revisions. Here there is no attempt to praise or blame, simply a desire to understand.

What follows from the basis of the argument itself leads to very much the same conclusions concerning our ability to reach truth as those actually set down by Bradley when he later stated his conclusions in the context of a detailed metaphysics and also, in sceptical import at least, as those stated here in the *Logic*. Truth can only be attained partially by any judgment. It develops toward the ideal limit of absoluteness, represented ultimately by the entire judgmental complex. Thus the truth inherent in any judgment is a function of the relation of that judgment to other judgments, the criterion being always the way in which the individual judgment coheres in the system of knowledge.

That Bradley's failure to trace the actual implications of his beliefs can be laid to his merging his "convenient" copy theory of truth with the notion that truth and existence are somehow one, can be evidenced by a few quotations. The copy theory was sufficient in itself to keep him from a proper development of his views, but the identification of truth with existence was partially responsible for his conclusions about the "validity of inference," despite the essentially similar conclusions that could be reached on the basis of the coherence theory that he should have developed.

In the section in which Bradley writes of degrees of truth, he uses the term "facts" in such a way that it is indispensable to the interpretation of the passage to ascertain its precise meaning. But from certain comments[51] it seems that "facts" has no one meaning; "facts" are sometimes taken to be those entities which are perceived, and sometimes these plus all entities perceivable in the past and in the future. The connection between judgment and fact is stated thus:

---

[51] *PL*, p. 74, among other places. We have already quoted Bradley's statement that he sought to "identify reality with the series of facts."

"A judgment, we assume naturally, says something *about* some fact or reality. If we asserted or denied *about* anything else, our judgment would seem to be a frivolous pretense. We not only must say something, but it must also be *about* something actual that we say it. For consider; a judgment must be true or false, and its truth or falsehood can not lie in itself. They involve a reverence to a something beyond. And this, *about* which or *of* which we judge, if it is not fact, what else can it be?"[56]

The above quotation is quite explicit that judgment is *about* fact; there is no mention of judgment *being* fact. Yet, in his discussion of modality, Bradley asserts: "There are no degrees of truth and falsehood. If S — P *is* fact, it can not *be* more than fact: if it *is* less than fact, it is nothing at all. The dilemma is simple. S — P is affirmed or it is not affirmed. If it is not affirmed, it is not judged true at all. If it is affirmed, it is declared to *be* fact, and it can not *be* more or less of a fact."[57] Here the language is equally clear that the truth or falsehood of a judgment consists in its *being* or not *being*, fact. It may be that I am trying to make a point on the basis of what is only linguistic convention, but Bradley is a careful writer and it is best to take him, literally, at his word.

V. The passages quoted are perhaps examples both of Bradley's refusal to acknowledge, from the beginning of the book, that discourse can be a counterpart of reality, and of his realization, during the course of his argument, that his theory of judgment is incompatible with a copy theory of truth. We are confronted, then, with three attitudes toward truth in the text of *The Principles of Logic:* (1) the theory that truth is a copy, injected "for the sake of convenience;" (2) the theory that truth is reality, or fact; and (3) the theory that truth is coherence, stemming from the consideration of judgment and inference and recognized implicitly in portions of the book, though never explicitly formulated.

VI. Reality, throughout the *Logic,* is in little better case than truth. To avoid metaphysical discussion Bradley was ready to treat reality as though it were fact, as though it were "presentation" (a word fraught with difficulty as he uses it). But at the same time every discussion of the consequences of his doctrines as they bear on reality takes him away from the meaning he had determined to employ when using the word. " . . . the real," he says, "which appears in perception, is not identical with the real just *as* it appears there. . . . It would belong to metaphysics to discuss this further,

---

[56] *PL*, p. 41, italics mine. Note the use of the phrase, "fact or reality."
[57] *PL*, p. 197, italics mine.

and we must here be content with a crude result. The real is what appears to me. The appearance is not generic but unique. But the real itself is *not* unique, in the sense in which its appearance is so.

"The reality we divined to be self-existent, substantial, and individual; but, as it appears within a presentation, it is none of these . . .

"The real can not be identical with the content that appears in presentation. It for ever transcends it, and gives us a title to make search elsewhere."[58]

There is evident throughout much that appears on the subject of reality in the book that Bradley's attempt to write a treatise on logic and his temptation to deal with the implications in metaphysical terms of the kind of logic that he found himself writing, resulted in a constant shift in the meaning of important terms. Yet he is careful that his ultimate conclusions, no matter what the reasons specifically urged for their adoption, be not too far removed from the conclusions that would have to be accepted if the metaphysical consequences of his doctrines were elaborated.

In one passage at the close of the final chapter, a selection justly famed for its eloquent intensity, he writes: "It may come from a failure in my metaphysics, or from a weakness of the flesh which continues to blind me, but the notion that existence could be the same as understanding strikes as cold and ghost-like as the dreariest materialism. That the glory of this world in the end is appearance leaves the world more glorious, if we feel it is a show of some fuller splendour; but the sensuous curtain is a deception and a cheat, if it hides some colourless movement of atoms, some spectral woof of impalpable abstractions, or unearthly ballet of bloodless categories. Though dragged to such conclusions we cannot embrace them. Our principles may be true, but they are not reality. They no more make that whole which commands our devotion, than some shredded dissection of human tatters *is* that warm and breathing beauty of flesh which our heart found delightful."[59] In a note on the use of the word "existence" as it occurs in this passage, Bradley comments: " 'Existence' is taken here widely in the sense of 'reality.' "[60] This note, however, was written in 1922 of something originally published in 1883. If "existence" is to mean "reality" and Bradley were consistent in his attempt to identify "reality" with the series of facts,

---

[58] *PL*, pp. 70, 71.
[59] *PL*, p. 591. Quoted by T. S. Eliot, *For Lancelot Andrewes,* p. 74f, as an example of Bradley's style at its best.
[60] *PL*, p. 595, note 28.

then it is obvious that "existence" would here mean the series of facts, which indeed is the chief use he makes of the word throughout the *Logic*. But if "existence" is to be taken "widely in the sense of 'reality'" the meaning may be different. Just what force "widely" is to have in this connection might be difficult to ascertain, but the high eloquence of the passage is sufficient to indicate that Bradley's terms are employed here as more than conveniences, and "existence" must have originally been taken to mean something like "reality" as Bradley later conceived it, rather than as the series of facts.

Granting such a meaning to the word "existence" as it appears above, the entire passage carries no implication that "existence" as the series of facts cannot be "the same as understanding." If Bradley's own statement as to the meaning of the word be accepted (and I think that, twenty-nine years after the publication of the book, Bradley would have written "the series of facts" rather than "reality" if that were what he meant), then this famous passage is not a rejection of the notion that judgment must somehow be fact, in order to be true. That judgments are in the realm of discourse rather than in that of existence (in the sense of fact) is, after all, the chief reason that Bradley urges against the possibility of their being true. He assumes that only a fact can be a copy of a fact, somewhat as Berkeley insists that only an idea can be like an idea. Unless on the basis of such an assumption I see no way to account for a typical passage such as the following: "This discursive nature of judgment and reasoning is fatal to their claim of copying existence. The process of the inference can never be true, and the result can never represent the fact."[61] Such an assumption seems, also, the only explanation, other than inconsistency, for the manner in which Bradley's argument shuttles between a theory of truth as a copy of existence and a theory of truth as identity with existence.

VII. Before turning to a consideration of the third theory of truth in Bradley's *Logic,* a theory implicit throughout, I should like to discuss briefly Bradley's treatment of analysis and synthesis, and of the abstract and the concrete, after which I shall try to point out the consequences of his conclusions for the theory of truth.

Analysis,[62] for Bradley, starts with some immediately apprehended whole and consists in an attempt to reduce it to its elements. In the course of the analytic process the relations between the elements are revealed and the process ends with the destruction of the confused whole and the statement, in its place, of a realm of abstract

---

[61] *PL,* p. 584.
[62] See *PL,* Book III, Part 1, Chapter VI.

connections. The laws of the whole are discovered and the conclusion may be regarded as a synthesis. On the other hand, synthesis as a method is characterized by starting with first principles, or axioms, and constructing from them an entire system for the subject matter. But this construction is really an analysis of the initial principles and it follows its proper course by moving to those elements of which the principles hold. So analysis and synthesis constitute one process. They may be regarded as different aspects of that process, but every act of reasoning involves both aspects. "Analysis is the synthesis of the whole which it divides, and synthesis the analysis of the whole which it constructs. The two processes are one."[63] Bradley's opposition to the contention that analysis was the sole method of philosophy rested on this statement of its relation to synthesis.

From the recognition that synthesis and analysis were basically one it followed, Bradley argued, that the more you analyze the greater the unity of your subject matter and the more you synthesize the greater its detail and hence its differentiation. This, he thought, should be substituted for the traditional and absurd doctrine that the extension of the subject matter varies inversely with its intention. That false doctrine he ascribed to the use of the abstract universal and the failure to understand the concrete universal which appears as the identity of analysis and synthesis.

The distinction between the abstract and the concrete is made as follows.[64] The real cannot be abstract, for it is substantial and individual. Since, however, an individual is not an ultimate simple, a purely atomic being, but rather an entity with a character, possessing an "internal diversity of content," it must be universal, meaning by that word "the identity of differences." This universal, not being abstract, is properly called "concrete." Taking "particular" to mean the atomic, that which contains no differences, it is clear that anything that is real and, hence, individual, is not particular. But any real, so long as it is in existence, is finite, and in that sense particular. So that, in its aspect as finite, the real may be called a "concrete particular," to distinguish it from the abstract particular, which is atomic.

The concrete universal and the concrete particular are individuals described in two ways. The former phrase is concerned with the universal aspect of the individual, its oneness despite the diversity of its content; the latter is concerned with the particularity of the individual, its difference from other individuals.

---

[63] *PL*, p. 471.
[64] See *PL*, Book 1, Chapter VI.

The methods of analysis and synthesis seem to be those which explore the individual as concrete universal by, respectively, starting with the diversity of content and analyzing until the basic structural relations which constitute its oneness are revealed, and, on the other hand, starting with the character of the individual insofar as it is a single entity, and developing into a consideration of the actual detail, or diversity, of its characteristics.

In addition to synthesis and analysis, there is one more fundamental element employed in all thinking.[65] And we may arrive at an understanding of this by reflection on what cannot be classified under the heading of either of these principles and, further, on what they imply concerning reality, insofar as they constitute methods for revealing the concrete universal. What has not been explained by the two principles so far discussed is "the leap of transition from the possible to the real," the inference from the considered individual to the real individual. "If for metaphysics," Bradley writes, "what is individual is real and what is real individual, for logic too the rational is individual and individuality is truth. And this is no paradox. Our practical criterion in every enquiry is the gaining all the facts and the getting them consistent. But this simple test unconsciously affirms that the individual is true and the truth individual. For a fragment of the whole broken off abruptly, or a whole that internally was at issue with itself, would alike fall short of individuality. Unawares then we strive to realize a completion, single and self-contained, where difference and identity are two aspects of one process in a self-same substance, and where construction is self-diremption and analysis self-synthesis. This idea of system is the goal of our thoughts, and to sight of this perfection we have been conducted."[66]

Analysis of any one element in this whole should end in the totality itself and so should be the internal development of a single portion. Synthesis, on the other hand, "would be the movement of the whole within its body,"[67] the exhibition of the entire system in each of its parts, and this would be a process whose culmination would be a return to itself, a kind of tour which would traverse the whole. Though this completed system be impossible of attainment it is, nonetheless, what would satisfy the intellect, and it shows what the third great principle of thinking is; self-development within and toward the whole.

VIII. The consequences of the above discussion for the theory of

---

[65] *PL*, p. 486f.
[66] *PL*, p. 487.
[67] *PL*, p. 489.

truth would consist in some doctrine of coherence. Had Bradley surrendered his original desire to use terms like "truth" and "reality" in what he regarded as an everyday sense in order to avoid metaphysical discussion, he might have developed immediately some of the consequences of the philosophy of logic and the epistemology with which he was filling his pages.

In accord with these consequences a few comments should perhaps be made as to the bearing on the nature of truth of these basic reflections on logic. Lest it be thought that Bradley's actual conclusions on this subject in his *Logic* differ essentially from those that would have obtained had he followed the implications of his own belief, it might be appropriate also to make some attempt to show why this is not the case.

The idea of self-development within a whole which is the completed system of all that can be said to be real involves the dependence of each part on all other parts and on the totality within which they are contained. And this should lead directly to coherence as the criterion of truth. Lack of coherence would then be contradiction in the sense of incompleteness. Here is a sceptical criterion fully developed, for anything short of the whole is so far lacking in reality, and utter consistency, or completeness, is itself the real. What remains to be shown is that any portion of the whole considered in itself is actually contradictory in the ordinary sense of being inconsistent. This becomes Bradley's task in the first book of *Appearance and Reality*.

The same conclusions can be attained from our previous considerations with respect to meaning. The manner in which truth is dependent on meaning is sufficient to insure that truth develops with meaning. The growth, then, of truth, is a function of the growth of a complex of judgments which can be said to constitute a system. Any individual judgment is dependent, for its truth-value as for its meaning, on every other judgment and, ultimately, on the system of which each is a part. It follows that truth is to be judged in terms of coherence rather than as a copy. And no single judgment can be completely true, as no single judgment can contain a complete meaning. Each judgment contains some degree of meaning and some degree of truth; equally it contains some degree of unmeaning and some degree of falsehood. These are to be found in judgments in all possible proportions. At this point there is some difficulty in being sure of our ground. Why must there be some degree of falsehood in a judgment that is only partially true? Is it not possible that, were the meaning of the judgment fully established, the judgment would be completely true, that it is only partially true because its full meaning has not been ascertained? Such an objection must fail because the meaning of every judgment is dependent on the system of judgments. In the same manner its truth, waiting on the full explication of its meaning, is only complete when the meaning is, i.e. in the entire judgmental complex. But why call a lack of such completion partial falsehood? Is not falsehood something entirely different. On this account, no. Falsehood is tantamount to incompletion. An explanation of this leads through still another consideration.

IX. If truth is dependent upon a system and if meaning, too, develops as the system nears completion and is completed with it, it might be interesting to discover the relation of truth and meaning. We have already noticed the dependence of truth on meaning, and are prepared to state that the growth in truth of a judgment is in direct proportion to the growth of its meaning. One important question concerning truth, on this account, is: how can a judgment, or group of judgments, thought to be true (in great part) ever come to be regarded as false (in great part)? Since truth is consistency, it is probable that the answer lies in the consistency or inconsistency of our judgment of judgments with the mass of accepted judgments in the field and with the body of knowledge at the time. A group of judgments may be accepted at some time but as other judgments are formed, as the result of investigation, both groups, admittedly consistent internally, must be compared to insure that they do not contradict each other. If a contradiction or inconsistency is discovered, and all attempts to eliminate it fail, that group is rejected which is in least harmony with the body of judgments composing our knowledge of the rest of the field. Should this alone prove insufficient (as would be the case if there were no other knowledge in the field or if both were equally consistent with our other knowledge) decision about them would be held in abeyance until further investigation yielded still more relevant judgments. The consistency of our new judgments with either of the groups under consideration would then determine the group to be accepted, and the other, which might have been the group originally thought to be true, would then be condemned as false.

In a case of this kind what can be said of the meaning of the judgments which were originally believed and which were later denied? Of the others it is easy to say that their development in truth was directly proportional to their development in meaning. But the first group lost its status in truth. Was there a corresponding loss in meaning? I think we can not refuse to answer affirmatively.

The original group of judgments, like all other such groups, contained meanings which were fuller and clearer than the meanings contained in the individual judgments composing it. As another group, inconsistent with the first, was formulated, the meanings contained in the two, taken together, dissolved in the crucible of contradiction. They simply cancelled each other out.

An assertion or a denial which is itself a contradiction is analytically false. But if it is understood as containing one idea, or meaning, and one only, then the statement is also meaningless. It might be asserted that, on any interpretation, it is meaningless. Certainly, on this one, it must be so. "This bald man has a full head of hair," apart from the artifices by which "we have our naked frailties hid," must be adjudged obviously false and contradictory, but the terms composing the judgment might be said to have meaning. On Bradley's view, the terms of this assertion would be elements in a composite idea, they would be tentatively fixed meanings in a fuller meaning. And the one "idea" present would be: "This bald man with the full head of hair."

Such a conjunction of words can scarcely be dignified by the appellation "idea." We are confronted with a series of words which convey no meaning since they contradict anything they might express. They are in the same case as the words composing the phrase "a square circle:" they cannot be said to signify anything.

A similar situation is apparent with regard to the two groups of propositions we considered before. Taken separately each group contains meanings, as each might on occasion be thought to contain truth. Taken together, they can contain meaning no more than they can contain truth. The inconsistency which robs them of the one at the same time deprives them of the other. The meanings which have been clarified and developed in each group come into fatal conflict with the meanings which have been clarified and developed in the other. If one group asserts "This is a bald man," the other group asserts "He has a full head of hair." And taken together what has been clarified and developed is the meaninglessness of our "ideas."

What we discovered must be done was to accept one group and to reject the other. We were prepared to do this since there could be no question of truth if we retained both; equally there could be no question of meaning. The group rejected must be denied meaning, not in itself, but if kept in the body of belief along with the other. The accepted group, on the other hand, does not lose its meaning because of the conflict; rather it retains the meaning yielded by its internal structure and then merges that meaning with the meaning of further judgments in the field. These fuller meanings are constantly in a stage of development unless still another group of judgments, incompatible with them, enters the field and emerges victorious.

What is meant by the assertion that a rejected group loses its meaning when kept in the body of belief along with an accepted group, is not intended to imply that both groups actually are or should be kept within the system of our beliefs. Only one is to be believed. But the other group may be compared with or contrasted to the believed group. And in such contrast it is meaningless, because contradictory. The accepted group actually has a place in the complex of judgments constituting our beliefs. The rejected group, *considered in itself,* contains a partial meaning, but it is a meaning that does not develop with the growth of our knowledge, since it is incompatible with that knowledge. So, as its erstwhile rival contributes its meaning to a larger system, within which it grows, this rejected group contains less and less meaning proportionately to that of the system from which it is excluded, and thus does not conform to the principle of self-development. It offers a static group of meanings which is beggared in comparison with the ever richer meanings of the body of knowledge in the field within which it was intended to function. And it cannot be, or represent, anything real since a real thing may even be defined as that which, on analysis, develops till it reaches the whole.

In still another sense the group which has been denied has lost meaning to a much greater extent. Insofar as it pretends to truth its pretension carries it within the boundary of our beliefs. It contends for a place within that system. And in this respect it must be considered, *not in itself,* but rather *in comparison with* the judgments which have received the acceptation which it has been denied. Viewed in this light, taken together with judgments with which it is inconsistent, it is as utterly meaningless as it can be in these terms.

There is still another general interpretation which can be placed on the process we have been considering and which is based on self-development. We have been speaking of one group of judgments as entering into the complex of belief because fresh judgments, formulated as a result of new investigation in the field, have all been consistent with it. The process can be understood fully as well if it is asserted that the group which is accepted is that group whose meaning is enriched and clarified by new judgments within its field; while the group that is rejected is one whose meaning is lessened by each fresh judgment within the field, since all such judgments contain meanings incompatible with it. The group which is permitted to enter as a portion of our belief is caught up in the web of meaning and increases in fullness and clarity as each fresh thread fills in the outlines or adds to the scope of the whole. The rejected judgments are those with which just such development is impossible. Perhaps, also, a completely rejected group of judgments could be shown, on analysis, to be contradictory in themselves, and so without meaning at all.

Without any reference to the latter interpretation it is possible to state the relation of the decrease in meaning to the decrease in truth by asserting that the decrease in the meaning of any judgment or judgments is directly proportional to its decrease in truth. The possibility of the second interpretation, however, or rather the realization that it makes no difference to an understanding of the process which interpretation is employed, aids us to identify, ultimately, truth and meaning in such a system. Meaning increases as truth increases and it decreases as truth decreases. Both judgments are, on the basis of our analysis, simply convertible. It seems further to be the case that all that can be said of either meaning or truth can with equal veracity be said of the other. This is, pragmatically at least, sufficient demonstration of their identity. And certainly if one term can, on all occasions, be substituted for another, without either loss or gain in the meaning or truth-value of the judgments within which such substitution is effected, then those terms are synonymous, for that is precisely what it means to be synonymous.

X. For some purposes it is more important to know what a man should have said, in terms of his initial assumptions, than to know what he did say. That, I think, is the situation here. The basic doctrines of *The Principles of Logic* give rise logically to a theory of truth and meaning as a system within which every judgment contains some degree of both and within which truth and meaning are interchangeable terms. The difficulties with which such a theory is beset need not be noted here because, for our purposes, it is more important to consider them in the light of the theory of truth which Bradley actually evolved, a theory similar in essentials to the one just propounded, which has a function of the highest importance in the metaphysical scheme of *Appearance and Reality*. And, to clarify the sceptical method employed in that book, we have considered the formation of a doctrine in which both truth and meaning are realized completely only in a whole which is all-embracing and consistent. Any part considered in itself is not, so far, to be accepted as real. It is up to Bradley to show that the incomplete is not self-consistent when considered apart from the total universe, for if any part could be thoroughly consistent it would no longer imply a whole which contains it. Parts would then be independently real and the whole would be a mere aggregate. But if every portion short of the whole can be shown to be contradictory, then they can neither be thoroughly meaningful nor thoroughly true; truth and meaning will depend on the totality and so, for the same reasons, will reality.

CHAPTER III

LOGIC — TERMINAL ESSAYS

1. INFERENCE

I. The tools of scepticism were forged by Bradley in the first edition of his *Principles of Logic*. It is the manner of that forging and the instruments forged that have been considered thus far, with some revisions of the second edition noted. Since the *Logic* was first published in 1883 and the second edition, containing the famous *Terminal Essays,* in 1922, it is evident that Bradley's writings on logic both precede and follow his *Appearance and Reality,* published in 1893, and his *Essays on Truth and Reality,* published in 1914. The content of the *Terminal Essays,* obviously, constitutes Bradley's final reflections on logic and cannot be said to form, insofar as it may differ from his earlier work, the entire basis of either the scepticism or the dogmatic philosophy of *Appearance and Reality*. Nonetheless, as I shall try to show later, Bradley's metaphysics is, in general, thoroughly consistent with his later logical doctrines, probably because the latter were formulated with the metaphysical system clearly in mind.

II. As it has been outlined so far Bradley's logic gave rise to a scepticism based chiefly on two points, which were fundamentally one: (1) discourse is essentially a system, the meaning, truth, and reality of whose parts is dependent upon a perhaps unattainable whole; (2) truth may be regarded, for the sake of "convenience," as a copy of reality, but otherwise it should be taken as identity with reality, and this thought can never be. It remained for Bradley to show that the relational nature of thought made comprehension of a non-relational whole impossible. The two sceptical conclusions stated above imply that for truth to be reality it must not only encompass, but actually become, the whole; the entire system of discourse must be the system of reality, for no part of the latter totality is real save for its dependence on the system which contains it. Since the whole is ultimate consistency there is one other important corollary; any part, taken in itself, is inconsistent, at least from the standpoint of the total context, so inconsistency, or contradiction, should provide a criterion for determining the unreal, as thorough consistency, or harmony, should suffice for determining the real.

Since Bradley's attempt to treat truth as a "copy," and reality as the "series of facts" resulted in a constant ambiguity in the use of those terms, forcing us to draw our conclusions from his specific analysis of other subjects, it is important to bolster and extend these conclusions in the light of his later account of logical matters, in which he gave up the "convenient" meaning of terms and no longer believed that any ideas could "float" absolutely.

III. The themes I wish to consider are included as portions of Bradley's treatment of inference, judgment, and negation, which I shall take in that order. Under the heading of inference, I shall restrict myself, chiefly, to three subjects: (1) the self-development of an object, (2) the dual nature of the subject, and (3) the solution provided by the first two of the problem of inference yielding new knowledge. In addition I shall, as ever, be concerned with the implications for scepticism of the material under consideration.

IV. The first of the *Terminal Essays*, which deals with inference, states on its first page: "Inference being a process, I will state at once what I take as its essential nature. This may be set down as the ideal self-development of an object."[1] The chief question in connection with this statement seems to turn on the meaning of the word "object." It is an "object" which develops itself ideally in inference, and that self-development constitutes the essence of the process of inference—but what kind of entity is this "object?" Merely to say it is an individual, or concrete universal, is not much help. The matter is perhaps confused further rather than clarified when the point is restated. "Every inference is the ideal self-development of a given object taken as real."[2]

The "given object" might, of course, be taken to mean the subject of an argument or, what is the same thing, the subject of its conclusion. There is development, to be sure, from the time the subject first occurs in a judgment during the course of the argument to the time it appears in the conclusion. And this development is certainly ideal since it takes place in discourse. But in what sense is it the ideal *self*-development of the object? Bradley's own identification of the "given object" may be of help at this point. "The given object," he says, "is an ideal content before us, taken to be real as being in one with Reality, the real Universe." If the object is an ideal content it can be only a meaning, and there is clearly a sense in which a meaning could undergo self-development in the course of inference: it is meaning that must develop *itself* in inference in that any other kind

---
[1] *PL*, p. 597.
[2] *PL*, p. 598.

of development would include some mental leap beyond the boundaries prescribed by the argument. But there is still to be explained the phrase "taken to be real as being in one with Reality, the real Universe."

The "object" with which inference is concerned is, we have seen, "ideal" in its development and, being thus ideal, may be regarded as a meaning (that is, if Bradley's earlier writings do not mislead us here), or, at least, as being a meaning in its inferential development. But it is also "taken as real." And that phrase is amplified when Bradley uses it again, later in the essay: "Now this object, like all objects, is taken, we may say, as referred to Reality, the real Universe; or, to speak more correctly, the object is taken as in one with this Reality."[3] So that another way, albeit less correct, of saying the same thing, is the assertion that the object "is taken as referred to Reality." Now it can scarcely be a meaning which Bradley thinks is referred to Reality, but rather that which it signifies. We seem to be concerned, then, with the development in meaning, in virtue of its own characteristics, of that which the meaning signifies, considered as a portion of the system of existence.[4] And this, I think, is but another way of stating the fundamental point that any judgment is to be understood as R (S-P). S-P being a statement of some one idea, the judgment must be interpreted as asserting that Reality is such that there can be this idea, or that there is this idea. Still another way of stating the same thing would be the assertion that Reality is of such a character that it contains that which is signified by the judgment. The actual subject of any judgment—the idea it exhibits—and the implicit subject—its reference to Reality—had not been considered with sufficient care in the *Logic* itself. Here in the *Terminal Essays* the statement of the nature of inference is made in such a manner that the dual nature of its subject can be treated more fully.

Before going on to treat this matter, some comment should be made of the object considered from the side of reality. We have learned, in the study of the *Logic* itself, that the reality which discourse attempts to reveal is an all-embracing system, the elements of which are individuals, or concrete universals. By the method of analysis an investigation of any of these individuals would disclose

---

[3] *PL*, p. 600.

[4] I use the word "system" in this connection because of Bradley's preference for the phrase "being in one with Reality" over his alternative "referred to Reality," a preference which, I think, is dictated by the connotation of the first phrase that something is contained in a whole, or system.

its connections with other individuals and would ultimately, if discourse could become complete, include the system of the whole. Some kind of development, then, could be said to take place in reality itself, a development of the individual by virtue of which it becomes the whole. This seems to be the meaning of Bradley's contention that the developing object should be "taken as real," or "as in one with Reality." But the individual has, in itself, taken part in no development. The development is that of the individual as idea. So that any element in Reality may be considered insofar as it functions in discourse, or, to put it otherwise, an idea is an individual insofar as that individual is thought.[5] And an individual may be treated in this manner, usually identified with neo-Realism, as the way in which it functions in discourse, or it may be treated simply as a portion of a Reality which transcends discourse. This is perhaps the basis of Bradley's distinction between appearance and Reality. It may be, also, that the individual is the idea embodied in any judgment, the separate terms of which are the detail, or differentiation, of its content. If so, what is an individual will vary from context to context, and any individual will be composed of others.

V. In an inference this object[6]—the subject of the judgment—develops. But the subject is both actual and implicit; it is both some special theme in Reality and the symphony of the whole. Does one or the other develop, or do both? That the actual subject is conceived as developing is obvious from what has gone before but that the implicit subject, Reality itself, is thought of as developing in the course of inference may well seem preposterous. On the other hand, since the special subject may be considered as being what it is from the beginning, the development in inference might be no more than the development of our knowledge. On this view, Reality, too, would have an ideal development, a development from what we had known about it on the basis of the premises to what we know about it in the conclusion. Bradley, however, does not seem to mean anything of this kind. The object, as exhibited in a judgment which is a premise, is not identical with the object exhibited in the judgment which is the conclusion of the inference. The conclusion represents a development of the object with which we started. It is not that there is an object which is stated in our conclusion which we have gradually apprehended by the process of inference but rather that we started with a less developed object and that that object developed in our inference into the object in our conclusion.

---

[5] This is expanded in Chapter VII: The Ideal and the Real.
[6] For another discussion of the "object", see *PL,* p. 73f.

The subject that developed was not Reality but some special portion of it. And that portion developed only because of its interconnections with other portions and, ultimately, the whole. The ability to develop which is contained in the actual subject is there only because of the implicit subject; that is to say, the actual subject is dependent on something for its development and that something is a system within which it has a place. It is the systematic interconnection of all things, their existence within Reality, that enables them to have an ideal development. This is the basis of the solution, in Bradley's terms, to the question of whether an inference is a mere tautology or whether its conclusion contains new knowledge.

VI. It is the problem raised by the term "self-development" that results in such a solution and that brings about the clarification of the dual nature of the subject. We have already made reference to "the essential puzzle of inference," the difficulty raised by the consideration that if the object does not advance from its starting-point, then there is no inference; and if it goes beyond itself, beyond its boundaries, then there is still no possibility of calling the process inferential. The same problem considered in the book itself concluded in a formula which was regarded as satisfactory *for logic,* the notion that "at present we need to regard our reasoning as simply a change in our way of knowing. . . . If, by altering *myself,* I so am able to perceive a connection which before was not visible, then my act conditions, not the consequence itself, but my knowledge of that consequence."[7] On this earlier explanation of Bradley's it should be correct to assume that the subject develops in both its aspects, for our knowledge of Reality would develop with the growth of our knowledge about any special object.

In his later consideration of the problem Bradley again makes it clear that he is offering a solution which is sufficient only for logic and does not pretend to be a metaphysical conclusion. But the terms of the solution are no longer the same. The emphasis is not on reasoning as "a change in our way of knowing," but rather on the systematic whole within which the object, as an integral portion of that whole, develops. "The general solution of the problem raised by the essence of inference is found, I think, so far as logic is concerned, in the double nature of the object. Every inference, we saw, both starts with and is confined to a special object. Now this object, like all objects, is taken, we may say, as referred to Reality, the real Universe; or, to speak more correctly, the object is taken as in one with this Reality. Hence

---
[7] *PL,* p. 554.

the object not only is itself, but is also contained as an element in a whole; and it *is* itself, we must add, only as being so contained. And the difference of the object from, and its essential identity with a whole beyond itself—a whole which logic takes as a system both ideal and real—is the key (so far as logic is concerned) to this puzzle of self-development. On the one side the special object advances to a result beyond the beginning, and yet its progress throughout is nothing beyond the intrinsic development of its proper being. For that which mediates and necessitates its advance is implied within its own self."[8]

Inference being essentially the ideal self-development of an object, that object can only be understood as the special one, and indeed, in this section, Bradley specifically mentions the development of that object alone. Reality does not develop in inference but is, rather, the context which makes that development possible. As such, all inference depends on it and the existence of inference implies the existence of a Reality of a certain character. Bradley does not actually have to make the point here; what he has shown is that for a theory such as his, the study of logic leads to the acceptance of a real Universe one of whose characteristics, perhaps the chief one, being that it constitutes a system. The necessity for conceiving the Universe as systematic in character is based on its use here as the sine qua non of inference. In order for us to be able to infer there would have to be a background of systematic interconnections within which our subject existed— for the object, it must be remembered, is always "taken as real." "Logic in a word assumes that *Implication* exists, and that implication, where genuine, is also real. It assumes the reality of an ideal Universe, and of subordinate wholes and systems within this Universe."[9]

VII. This is the first use of the word "implication" in the entire *Principles of Logic*[10] and it makes its entrance with all the fanfare of italics and with its initial letter capitalized. It is implication that logic assumes, since inference consists in the development of an object and that development implies a system of connections, a system the name for which seems to be "implication." Logic also "assumes the reality of an ideal Universe." The universe of discourse, that is, can no longer be thought of as a counterpart of the real; it actually is real. But that is not to say that discourse is Reality. To be real is to be "taken as in one with Reality," to be, in other words, some por-

---

[8] *PL*, p. 599f.
[9] *PL*, p. 600.
[10] Save for the notes in the Second Edition.

tion of the whole which is Reality itself. Discourse on this account is, as I understand it, the system of special subjects, or individuals, all of which are integral portions of Reality, and are ascribed to it in every judgment. This is not the same as being the system of the whole within which all special subjects are contained. Only if discourse were complete and perfect would it be Reality itself.

Here the sceptical import of Bradley's logical doctrines is clarified. Truth would have to be defined, in these terms, not merely as identity with the real, if that is regarded as a name for the elements of the whole, but as identity with Reality. If Reality were to mean the entire system of individuals in the Universe in their relations to each other, truth would perhaps be theoretically possible but it would be highly improbable that it could be attained; but if Reality is to mean something transcending the individuals that compose it, then it would be impossible of attainment. Since the latter is Bradley's meaning it is incumbent on him to exhibit in more detail the connection between truth and Reality, when he formulates an explicit metaphysic.

To summarize what Bradley has to say about development by quoting his own words: " . . . where you have a system, you can, starting at a given point within the system, develop this by a necessity which is the real intrinsic nature of your beginning. The necessity belongs to your special object itself, not although but because it is at the same time beyond your object, and because it qualifies at once that object and the whole system in which the object has its place. And, while the above assumption is, perhaps, in the end, indefensible, it is here, I submit, that logic has to find an answer to its inherent puzzle of self-development."[11]

2. JUDGMENT

I. In treating the subject of judgment in the *Terminal Essays*, Bradley's emphasis falls on its relation to inference, a theme stated clearly enough in the *Logic* itself but without great detail. The essence of his theories as originally stated was, as we have seen, that judgment, idea, and inference constituted a system within which each was to be distinguished more as an aspect of the whole than as a part within it. This doctrine, implicit in the entire argument, received very little explicit formulation. As it is handled in the essay *On Judgment* it is fundamentally a realization of the consequences of his initial assumptions. In addition to examining Bradley's elaboration of this material I shall here consider at some length the meaning of the two aspects of the subject in judgment.

---

[11] *PL*, p. 600f.

II. Judgment, Bradley insists, cannot properly be considered a statement of some *"mere* fact," a completely unmediated, directly apprehended state of affairs. Always it carries with it reference to context, always it implies mention of Reality. Whenever there is the judgment "S is P," there is really the judgment "Reality is such that S is P." This being the reiteration of his original starting-point, it seems evident that what is to follow is regarded by Bradley as the consummation of this view.

In the judgment "Reality is such that S is P," the word "such" is understood to mean that there is "something" in Reality which is the ground for S being SP. The form "S is P" which means the same thing, nonetheless contains no actual mention of the "something," the ground. As such, the judgment may be regarded as different from that which explicitly states the ground, i.e., the inference. "On the other side, what you have gained, when you thus insist on the simplicity of your judgment, is no real matter of fact but in effect and truth a sheer abstraction. Hence, if this is so, every judgment will imply an inference essentially. Judgment comes short of inference only so far as it omits to mark or specify a condition fundamental to its own being. Inference on the other side makes ostensible this condition involved in all judgment. It is hence (we must say) judgment developed; though, so long as the condition is not fully specified, the development remains imperfect. But a mere judgment, we have seen, is no more than an abstraction, which lives solely in and through our one-sided emphasis and our failure to observe."[12]

The use of abstractions may be important for purposes of discourse, and Bradley, certainly, would not want to forbid them; but to forget that they are abstractions would be, in the light of Bradley's emphasis, to court error too ardently. Judgment, considered apart from inference, is an abstraction. And what shall we say about inference apart from judgment? Inference is compound of judgments; it is, considered in itself, a process without content, the mere skeleton of our reasoning. Bradley's emphasis on the whole is so great that, as one expects in such an attitude, he sees its components as deriving their very being from participation in the larger context. Judgment, idea, and inference are, indeed, not only components of one process; they are aspects of that process, what we see when we view the whole from one standpoint or another.[13]

---

[12] *PL*, p. 624f.
[13] This treatment of judgment and inference is, as we shall see, an analogue of the treatment of appearance and reality. The discussion of idea, judgment, and inference, further, constitutes an analogue of the three levels of reality.

III. The contention that any judgment essentially implies an inference, but that the judgment is ordinarily in such guise as to conceal this, its true character, may, of course, be extended to ideas, which are, for Bradley, always expressed as judgments, if they are expressed at all. "Judgment and idea, though, like inference, the same always in essence, may be taken, like inference at various levels. And, so taken, they may differ in form and may bear a varying sense. They may be explicit and offer themselves as judgment and idea; or again, while it is there in substance, they may fail to make this character ostensible. Thus, wherever you have an object, you can speak of judgment and idea as being present essentially, since you have here an idea referred to reality, and in a sense affirmed as true. For an object, as an object, implies and means a content at once distinguished from and taken as belonging to the whole remaining Universe. And, since with the selection of such a content its existence otherwise is ignored, the object already is ideal, and, with this, you have at once idea and judgment."[14] On the other hand, insofar as a perceived object is not, actually, "affirmed as true," judgment, though present essentially, is not present explicitly and in the strict, or logical sense, merely because something is perceived it is not, ipso facto, a judgment.

IV. Where a perceived object is consciously referred to reality, judgment, in its limited sense, can be said to exist. Any judgment, as has been remarked at some length in the consideration of inference, has a two-fold subject, special and ultimate; or, to use Bradley's language on certain occasions, it has reference to both a selected and a residual reality. If one bears in mind Bradley's insistence that in judgment but one idea is expressed, he encounters here a real difficulty. Although in any sentence there may be both subject and predicate, the judgment which it expresses cannot, if we take seriously the contention that there is only one idea present, contain either subject or predicate as they are stated in the sentence. The real subject, according to Bradley's original view, must be Reality and the predicate must be SP, the combination of the subject and predicate of the sentence. If the subject is said to be two-fold, it is difficult to understand what the predicate would be; for the special subject would be the subject term of the sentence and the predicate could scarcely be the predicate term, since that would confuse the doctrine that the entire judgment constitutes a predicate of the ultimate subject. On such an understanding there would be two ideas in the judgment and Bradley's doctrine of the dual nature of the subject would mean that there are two ways

---

[14] *PL*, p. 626.

of interpreting a judgment: first, as it is conventionally interpreted; second, as containing but one idea which it refers to Reality. In one of the notes in the second edition of the *Logic,* Bradley writes, of his statement that every judgment contains but one idea: "This statement requires correction. It is true that the ideal meaning is one; but it is also true that the subject is a special subject, and that it, in its special sense, must be there within the meaning. The twofold nature of Reality as the subject of judgment was not sufficiently recognized by me."[15]

The correction, I submit humbly, is somewhat ambiguous. Bradley is correcting what he wrote despite the fact that it is true. If he erred by not adding something essential to his account, his addition of it in the note does not help matters fundamentally. There is still the difficulty of understanding whether, from the standpoint of the special subject, there is but one idea in a judgment. But at least one thing is made clear. The emphasis on the special subject does not preclude, but rather complements, the doctrine of the single idea. That means that even where the subject is regarded as the special one, the judgment contains only the one idea. And the traditional understanding of the judgment would not, in any case, be permissible.

A more careful analysis of Bradley's correction forces it, I think, to yield its meaning. "It is true," he says, "that the ideal meaning is one." In that respect he retains the position stated in the first edition of his *Logic*. There is not, indeed, any shift in doctrine; there is merely a new emphasis. Something had not been *sufficiently* recognized. " . . . it is also true that the subject is a special subject, and that it, in its special sense, must be there within the meaning." The word "also" bulks large in importance. That there is a special subject which, as such, is contained in the meaning, is a truth *in addition to* the truth that there is one and only one ideal meaning in every judgment. The statement about the special subject is not a portion of the truth about the one meaning; it is *also* true. The one meaning contained in every judgment may be symbolized as SP. That to which it is referred is Reality. So, in a sense, Reality is the subject of the judgment and SP the predicate. But there is also a special subject which the meaning exhibits. And here we may inquire into that which Bradley had not sufficiently recognized: "the twofold nature of Reality as the subject of judgment." Can this be taken to mean that there is but one subject, Reality, and that this subject must be taken in two senses? Certainly the entire tenor of Bradley's analysis seems to make such inter-

---

[15] *PL,* p. 39, note 14.

pretation the obvious one. But far more is involved. Reality, as it is referred to in a judgment, may have two meanings, special and ultimate, selected and residual. But what is the special, or selected, Reality? Is it the S term of the sentence? Such is often the answer given. Yet, if we accepted that answer we would have to admit that Bradley wants to interpret every judgment in two ways: first, as containing but one idea, which is referred to Reality; second, as containing two ideas, one of which is the subject and one the predicate. And, indeed, there is no escaping the conclusion that, if the selected Reality is the S term, there is another term left over of which there has been no account, unless that term is to be regarded as the predicate.

An interpretation such as that given above cannot, as we have already contended, be accepted as expressing Bradley's meaning. "It is true that the ideal meaning is one," he says, thus closing forever the doors to any interpretation which includes any mention of two or more ideas within the judgment. One might examine this very statement of Bradley's for loopholes, but they would be difficult to find. Of course the word "idea" is not used but idea and meaning may be regarded as synonymous in the account of judgment and inference. Bradley is quite explicit about that from the first chapter of the *Logic* on. Another possibility might come to light by examination of the phrase, "ideal meaning;" an attempt might be made to discover whether there is any basis in Bradley's book for a distinction between meanings that are ideal and those that are not. But I fear that "ideal meaning" is evidence only for the statement that even masters of English prose are redundant at times.

There is another difficulty in what has been said of Bradley's meaning. Even in understanding what was meant by the contention that every judgment contained one idea we were able to distinguish subject from predicate and so have, in effect, two ideas. If, in the assertion "Reality is such that S is P," Reality is the subject, then there is certainly a sense in which SP is the predicate. If every judgment involves reference to Reality, what is predicated of Reality is not Reality itself, for that would be tautologous, but something other than Reality, at least in the sense in which a portion of the whole is other than the whole. As a result it is possible to accuse Bradley of being unable, in essence, to escape from a subject-predicate logic. But there is also the possibility that there is a way of understanding Bradley's words which would justify his claims.

Since there is to be only one idea in every judgment and since the subject of a judgment is always Reality, selected Reality and residual Reality, it might be contended that by the word "subject" Bradley means the content of the judgment as that is properly understood. The content of the judgment being one idea, that idea may justly be called its subject. Using the word in this way it is, of course, folly to assert that to say a judgment has a subject is to imply that it has a predicate as well. The subject, Bradley asserts, has a dual nature, and it is this dual nature that constitutes the crux of his explanation of the "essential puzzle of inference," and that occupies, in the course of many different analyses, so many pages of the *Terminal Essays*. By a simple transposition of words we have here the statement that the content of a judgment, the single idea it exhibits, is dual in character. This subject, or content, is always Reality, so that all possible judgments contain statements of two kinds about Reality, or statements about two kinds of Reality; this and nothing more. The content of the judgment, in the light of our discussions heretofore, is both some individual, some real (and so is Reality in the sense of a selected content within it), and Reality as a whole (in the sense in which apprehension of any portion of the whole always involves a recognition of its total context).

The special subject of the judgment, thus understood, can no longer be regarded as its S term. It is rather the single idea expressed by the judgment which is to be regarded as its special subject—not S but SP. This is the "given object" whose ideal development Bradley regards as the essence of inference. Recognition of this does away with the notion that Bradley somehow was not consistent in rejecting the doctrine that a judgment contains more than one idea. If the special subject is SP there is no possibility that Bradley held to a more conventional interpretation of the judgment in addition to the interpretation expounded at the beginning of the *Logic*.

V. In the light of the above it is possible to understand more fully the meaning of the dual nature of the subject. It is not only true that all our thinking contains reference to Reality, that every object of thought is taken as being "in one with Reality;" it is also true that every content of thought is dependent upon Reality as a whole for its character, and thus for its existence as well. This we have said before. But now the implications of such a doctrine should be clearer. The content of thought is always Reality, some specific portion of Reality and the whole system of Reality within which it has its place. The phrase "residual Reality" which Bradley used to refer to the whole of which the "selected Reality" is but a part, is not a felicitous coinage. One tends to think that "residual Reality" is a residue, what is left over after the "selected Reality" has been subtracted; it is rather the whole of Reality taken as a system whose structure makes inference possible, for it makes possible the ideal development of the "selected Reality." Every judgment actually exhibits a single idea, SP, which is ideal in that it is thought, and is "in one with Reality," the system of the whole in that it is a real individual. There is, thus, no predicate and, in the conventional meaning of the word, no subject. It might be urged that the reference to Reality means that something is predicated of it but that would be mere verbal argumentation, since the very exhibition of some idea in a judgment involves that reference, and one cannot speak unless it is present.

VI. These reflections on the meaning of the judgment constitute the axioms of a theory of knowledge in the English tradition, for they begin with a consideration of ideas. What Bradley has done is, to be sure, also in keeping with the Idealist tradition, of which he is so worthy an inheritor. Logic and epistemology were regarded by him as organic, rather than atomic (if I may be permitted the use of two sadly overworked words). Knowledge, for him, began with judgment and inference, not with what Locke called ideas. But the word "idea," in a refined sense of the same meaning, became, for the consideration of knowledge, a synonym of judgment. And, as judgments, ideas became the materials of knowledge. Further, they were defined as the symbols of Reality, the terms in which we think about the whole and, at the same time, objects "taken as real."[16] Ideas (what Bradley calls by that name in his later logical writings) are objects of thought and these objects are selected portions of Reality, dependent on Reality as a whole for being what they are. There is, of course, no notion of a psychical entity contained in Bradley's use of the word "idea;" it is taken simply as a sign, as a "universal meaning." As a sign it is the object of thought which, by its nature, stands for a system of interconnections and, ultimately, for Reality (at least as an ideal limit of its process of self-development). Insofar as the object of thought is real it must be a portion of the system of Reality; and it follows that contemplation of an object contains implicit apprehension of the whole within which it exists. A single idea, therefore, any single idea, is the knowledge of some special object within Reality and the recognition that it has a place within the system of the whole. The dual nature of the subject and the dual nature of the idea are the same, for subject and idea are one.

VII. If the idea were less than the recognition of the "undivided totality" within which any selected object has its existence, if it were

---

[16] How ideas can be both these things is a problem depending for its solution on the relation of appearance to Reality. This will be treated in some detail later.

merely apprehension of the object itself, it would be a sheer abstraction, unworthy to enter the living structure of thought. Such recognition, and with it a realization of the dependence of the object upon its context of Reality, constitute a more advanced stage in the apprehension of the idea. This advance, or refinement, is the characteristic which distinguishes judgment from idea and constitutes, indeed, the only difference between the two. It is a difference in understanding rather than a difference in essence. The dependence of the selected on the residual Reality is, when noted and made explicit, the distinguishing characteristic of inference. So judgment and inference, too, differ in what is understood, what is made explicit, rather than in essence. "We have seen so far that, as every inference is a mediated judgment, so all judgment, being mediated really, is an inference. There is no difference between the two except that judgment, as such, is not mediated ostensibly. In what we call a mere simple judgment there is no appearance of a 'must' or 'because.' But the 'because' (we have seen) is there essentially, however much it is slurred or ignored. Our simple judgment in short is an abstraction, the mere creation of false theory, which only by an error can be accepted and be set up as an actual fact."[17]

The question of the dependence of the special object upon its ultimate context is raised by consideration of the "such" in the proper form of the judgment, "Reality is such that S is P." In still another statement of the relation of judgment to inference Bradley raises the point. "A judgment then (we have so far seen) is always conditioned. It is in every case mediated, though not always explicitly and formally. Everywhere its genuine affirmation is that 'Reality is such that S is P,' and certainly in this 'such' we have a real 'because.' Hence inference is no more than developed and explicated judgment, while judgment already on its side is inference, substantially, though not in actual form."[18]

"Reality is such that S is P" becomes "S is P because of the structure of Reality." A statement of what it is in Reality that is specifically responsible for S being P is an explanation of the ground on which we are entitled to assert the single idea "SP." This would constitute an explication of the precise dependence of each idea on the whole and the ground itself would be always and everywhere that whole. "The question 'What is because?' asks (I understand) about the nature of a 'ground.' And the 'ground' of a thing I take as that, both within the thing and beyond it, which makes it to be what it is.

---

[17] *PL*, p. 632.
[18] *PL*, p. 638.

Hence on one side (at least on my view) there can not conceivably be a ground and 'because' which is merely external. If the ground is not implied and so intrinsic, it, as a ground, has no meaning. On the other side, unless the ground is *beyond*, it, once more and no less, is meaningless. And for anything to imply merely itself is, to my mind, nonsense.

"The result of the above (to advance rapidly) is that the ground is a whole, in which the thing to be grounded must be included. It is a whole pervaded essentially by connection and implication, and is, in some sense, a system which throughout justifies its contents."[19] The ground on the basis of which anything can be asserted rationally is the entire system of discourse, the totality of judgments. The ground which is the support for any object, which provides it with the character it exhibits, is the whole system of Reality.

VIII. Perhaps it is this doctrine of dependence on the whole that constitutes the essence of Bradley's scepticism. Acceptance of such a belief commits one to a theory of degrees of truth, for the more complete, the closer to the whole, anything is, the truer it is. These degrees may approach but can never attain perfect truth, that which is beyond degrees, for that would consist in complete knowledge of everything and, in accordance with Bradley's contention that to be true is to be real, no one could be said to have such knowledge unless he somehow possessed the whole (perhaps in the sense of experiencing it).

An understanding of the twofold nature of the subject in all judgment is important for an understanding of what Bradley thinks can be known. The special subject, presumably, is the particular object of knowledge and, as such, must be known. The condition for such knowledge is a whole of which the special subject is a part. It must be assumed, then, that there is such a whole and that it has certain general characteristics, such as constituting a system, containing all things, etc. So that our knowledge is not only of the part but of the whole as well. On the other hand, to know more about Reality than these general characteristics would be to have all knowledge, which is impossible. But the knowledge we have of other things is dependent upon a completed system of discourse and can never be thoroughly true until the attainment of that system. So, from the standpoint of the whole, knowledge of a special subject would only be partial. Whether what can be known of the whole is in better case will be a future consideration.

IX. In the earlier *Logic* Bradley made a distinction between the

---

[19] *PL,* p. 633.

conditioned and the conditional[20] which he repeats and clarifies in the *Terminal Essays*. The conditioned is distinguished, he wrote, by the word "because"; the conditional by the word "if." The identification of the conditioned with the ground, which he seems to have had in mind at the time of his earlier writing, has been fully stated in the passage last quoted. But this identification is not complete. "Because" is a word which may be followed by a complete or a partial ground. Where complete it should be always the same: the connected whole on which the object depends; where partial it differs in accordance with the object: it is that portion of the ground which has been selected for mention. The condition is not the ground as such; it is some selected portion of the ground. " . . . what . . . is a 'condition'? A condition appears . . . to be a partial ground. Where anything is included in a whole which is its ground, there any other part of the ground, beyond this thing itself, is called its condition. And this element will be one among our thing's many conditions, unless at least we can assume or show that no further element is contained in the ground.

"Hence the 'because' of anything may be called that by which it is conditioned. Its full 'because' implies the presence of the entire whole of its conditions, and includes in this whole the thing's own nature, so far as grounded. This, and no less than this, is the true and real 'because.' But we can use 'because' again in a less complete sense where we take the thing as conditioned partly. Here we single out and refer merely to one selected element, one part of the whole of those connections which are involved in the ground. Such an imperfect use of 'because' is unavoidable and necessary in practice, but, indefensible in the end, it is even in practice a constant source of grave and insidious error."[21]

The ground and the condition are not exactly the same; both are included in the meaning of conditioned, but the condition is only some portion of the ground. The object itself is a portion of its own ground, since it participates in the whole in which it is grounded, but the object is not included in its condition, since that is "any other part of the ground."

In considering the conditional rather than the conditioned, we are concerned with a supposal rather than a supporting ground. A judgment which is conditioned by a full ground is a judgment which actually is mediated. "S here is P because of M. We had, in other words . . . , a whole which includes and supports and guarantees at once S

---

[20] *PL*, p. 99f.
[21] *PL*, p. 633f.

and P and also their actual junction. This is what is implied, and this is what we should mean when we call a judgment condition*ed*."[22] It seems clear that the mediation is here supplied by the M, which is the ground. "Now, where we employ 'if,' and where our judgment becomes condition*al*, we still always must have a necessary mediation and a 'because.' In 'S, if M, is P' the actual connection M-P is positively asserted, and M-P is taken as grounded and as unconditional. And, if we are unable to say that much, the entire judgment is ruined. Hence, wherever we use 'if' we must necessarily imply a 'because' on which our judgment depends. And our judgment 'S, if M, is P,' no matter how condition*al*, must also so far be condition*ed*.

"Thus, so far as 'M-P' is concerned, the above judgment is conditioned; but it is otherwise when we take the connection of S with M. Here we do *not* assert or assume conditions which to our knowledge connect S to M and so guarantee their union. On the contrary, our 'if' admits that the connection S-M remains in part unknown. We have hence asserted S-P subject to, and at the risk and mercy of, an unknown condition; and our judgment, therefore, as a whole, is merely conditional."[23]

The meaning of the above passage seems to be that, M being the ground (and without a ground there would be no judgment at all), P is conditioned by it and the connection M-P may be asserted positively. This is implied by the form "S, if M, is P," since, if S-M may be asserted, it would only follow that S-P could be asserted on condition that M-P were the case. Thus P is grounded, and S-P may be asserted only if S is also grounded, and grounded in a certain manner. But "S, if M, is P" does not imply that S is so grounded, nor that it is grounded at all. It does not even, that is, imply that there is an S. And the manner in which a judgment is grounded is properly to be expressed as "S, if M, is P" for it can merely assert a certain connection of attributes such that the idea SP is exhibited if there is an S and if S enters appropriately into that connection. Bradley perhaps assumes the existence of S or regards it as irrelevant but the manner in which S is grounded is regarded as crucial. "Certainly, (at least to me) S is *somehow* connected with M *in such a way that, taken so*, S remains itself. If our judgment, 'S, if M, is P' implies that S and M are united *somehow*, that judgment still does not assume that they are connected either simply or *anyhow*. To gain the required union with M, S (for anything our judgment knows) has to become something more and something else. It must be altered (for all we know) so

---

[22] *PL*, p. 634.
[23] *PL*, p. 634.

that, as such and as S, it is really no longer there. And the admission of this doubt surely is not compatible with the assertion that S is P because it is M. If that assertion is to stand it must be based on a ground assumed or known actually (we need not know *how*) to guarantee the connection S-M. Such a ground clearly, I repeat, is not involved in our judgment that S, if M, is P. And the replacement of this ground by an uncertain condition, the effect of which upon S is unknown, is, I urge, precisely that meaning of 'if' which separates 'if' from 'because.' "[24]

X. The notion of the conditional as a factor in all judgment brings this analysis of Bradley's to the conclusion reached by all his other analyses, that ultimately one must preserve a scepticism with regard to the possibility of attaining truth. Any attempt to ground S may result in the assertion of an idea S-M which may not contain as a portion of itself the original S in a completely unmodified form. And, in that we cannot ever be sure that this is not the case, we can never be sure that our judgment is true. It is the form of the judgment itself, Bradley would have us realize, that implies conditions that, perhaps, can never be realized. Of course the judgmental form with which Bradley confronts his readers is the result of the particular set of assumptions with which he commenced his logical investigations. Our own inquiry was intended to trace the manner in which those assumptions developed and to provide an example of sceptical conclusions arising from premises which are fundamentally sceptical.

Bradley's explicit conclusion to this line of investigation is, as one would expect, a reiteration of the scepticism to which he had been led by the argument of the first edition of the *Logic*. "We are ready, now at length, to ask whether all judgments are not only conditioned but also in the end conditional; and this question has perhaps by now been answered already. With every judgment we fail more or less to include its conditions within itself, and, with every judgment in the end, we do and we can not completely know what the entire conditions are. The 'such' in our 'Reality is such that', remains in the end and in detail not wholly knowable. Hence in our result we are unaware of the extent to which our S has really been modified. We can not tell how far it has been or may have been altered, or how far that alteration affects itself and M. There is a question therefore as to whether the necessary identity of S throughout the judgment has been maintained. And, since this question remains in the end unanswered, every judgment in the end is no more than conditional."[25]

---

[24] *PL*, p. 635.
[25] *PL*, p. 639.

If the S in the idea S-M is in any respect different from the S in the idea S-P, the validity of the judgment is destroyed. It may be objected that this is in reality only the contention that we can never be sure of eliminating the fallacy of four terms; and that four terms is properly a fallacy of inference, not of judgment, since it is a fallacy of argument rather than of assertion. This would be a legitimate criticism, to be sure, if we were talking of judgment in some other sense, but it is totally irrelevant here. Perhaps the chief point in Bradley's discussion of judgment is that it is implicit inference and it follows that it should be treated as such. This is in itself a sceptical principle because it implies a dependence of judgment and inference on each other, such that only in a completed system of judgments whose parts are inferentially connected, can there be complete truth.

Bradley's broader sceptical principles follow swiftly on the heels of the passage just quoted. "The growth of our knowledge consists in a widening and in an increase of systematic mediation. The more the conditions of the judgment are, or can be, included in the judgment, the truer and more real, the less condition*al* and more condition*ed* does that judgment become. And the judgment that seeks to be at once true and at the same time a mere simple and unconditioned assertion of fact, implies the worship and the pursuit of an illusory abstraction. It involves the assumption of a false and perverted ideal of knowledge. Such a judgment, the more it attempts to assert itself as absolute, succeeds only the more in emphasizing itself as dependent on and subject to the unknown. On the other hand, a system of knowledge where all judgment and inference would at once each be the other and be perfect, is in detail unattainable. It remains an ideal, genuine and to be realized actually more and more, but never completely."[26]

The entire structure of the system of knowledge as Bradley understands it is suggested in the above by the words "all judgment and inference would at once each be the other." The system of knowledge is fated forever to be imperfect but it approaches perfection as its judgments become inferences, i.e. as the grounds signified by the words "such that" in every judgment become explicit. From the standpoint of perfection there is, then, no distinction between judgment and inference, both, in principle, having the same form.

In conclusion it might be mentioned that there is one obvious criticism that can be made of Bradley's enterprise as a whole, a criticism which can be applied equally to certain others among Idealist philosophers. Rational thinking, he says, is a matter of judgment and infer-

---

[26] *PL*, p. 639.

ence and must, in the end, be acknowledged as sadly limited because judgment and inference, by their very natures, are barred eternally from the realm of truth. " . . . a system of knowledge where all judgment and inference would at once each be the other and be perfect, is in detail unattainable." If this be the case, under what conditions could any one ever know it, or, to pursue our figure a little further, by what magic is one able to open the close-locked portals, so unyielding before the onslaught of reason, in order that he may learn all this? If judgments and inferences cannot yield truth about anything, how can they yield truth about themselves? One possibility, of course, is the answer that Bradley's analysis of judgment and inference is itself to be accepted tentatively. Another is an appeal to some theory of types, in this case an appeal beset by more logical hazards than most thinkers would like to brave. Or, finally, there might be some means of attaining Bradley's conclusions other than that of employing judgments and inferences in the normal manner, perhaps by reflection on the incomplete system of discourse which they themselves constitute. If the third answer be offered it is Bradley's metaphysics that must justify it. But some explanation there must be or Bradley is left in the uncomfortable position of that Epimenides who spoke so unkindly of his fellow Cretans.

3. THE NEGATIVE JUDGMENT

I. The contention that all judgment qualifies Reality, that the expression of every idea is an expression of the structure of the real, can not be completely established unless some mention is made of negation. The negative judgment would seem to be an exception to such a doctrine, an assertion that here is something which does not hold of Reality, an explicit disavowal that this idea is "in one with Reality."

In this section I shall consider (1) the way in which negation is implied in all judgment, (2) the diversity in unity that is implied by this, (3) the disavowal of subjectivity in connection with the negative judgment, and (4) the way in which, on the basis of the foregoing, all ideas qualify Reality.

II. Bradley's doctrine of negation is entirely consistent with his analysis of judgment as such. In the sixth of the *Terminal Essays* he confesses error in his understanding of the negative judgment as expressed in the first edition of the *Logic*. The negative judgment qualifies the real as directly as does the affirmative judgment. More than that, every judgment contains within itself negation and disjunction. Although the form does not exhibit it, any judgment, by selecting some idea, implicitly distinguishes it from all others. The context of the judgment is a whole within which the judgment itself exhibits one idea, different, by the nature of the case, from everything else within the whole. "Thus every judgment is in essence, though not explicitly, both negative and disjunctive. And disjunction within a whole is the one way in and by which in the end negation becomes intelligible."[27]

Although this is the case essentially it is not the case explicitly, unless one so fully understands the connections of the idea he expresses that he makes actual mention of specific disjunctions and negations. Even where this is not the case there is awareness of the negation implied. "When in an early judgment I say 'Here is this,' and so select one feature from the universal mass, I do not of course explicitly deny that which my judgment neglects. I do not, that is, in putting 'this' on one side of my world, consciously place any 'that' on the other and excluded side. On the contrary I emphasize one element in my whole while disregarding the residue. But this residual mass, none the less, is there, and is actually experienced. And hence, even at this stage, I am in some sense positively aware of a totality which includes in itself both an aspect emphasized and an aspect ignored."[28]

A more precise statement of Bradley's position is perhaps to be found in the following selection: "Negation everywhere has a ground, not on one side merely but on both sides. There is a reason, a positive character, on account of which 'this' excludes 'that,' and 'that' again on its side is opposite to 'this.' There is no such thing as a distinction which, merely adventitious, supervenes wantonly, or is superimposed in the absence of a ground. And thus distinction and negation determine and qualify, even if in the end we can not everywhere show how precisely they do so. And it is useless to urge that, where we start with a mere ignoring of a residue, or where we are confined to a bare exclusion, the selection upon a ground, in at least such a case, is obviously not there. Such objections mistake, I would repeat, a mere abstraction for given fact. For where we distinguish in effect, and where we in any sense experience some element as at once present and ignored, we are already above the stage of bare exclusion, if indeed anywhere that could exist. And a distinction grounded on no difference may certainly be called a monster incapable of life except within a one-sided theory."[29]

The entire account of the negative judgment comes to rest, as does everything else in Bradley's logic, in the whole of Reality. Only in terms of the whole or, if you like, in terms of context, can every judg-

---

[27] *PL*, p. 662.
[28] *PL*, p. 663.
[29] *PL*, p. 664.

ment be understood as at once disjunctive and negative, even where in form it is affirmative. In the explanation of negation Bradley makes his fullest statement of the "diversity in unity" exhibited by every judgment. The unity is, of course, Reality, the identical element in all judgment; the diversity is the disjunction implied by the very notion of selection, the particular idea expressed set off against the residue.

III. In respect of "diversity in unity" the system of discourse, which is a system of meaning, the system of ideas exhibited, is one way of describing the system of existence, as it is in so many other respects. The very notion of Reality receives an extension in the treatment of the negative judgment. This will perhaps be clearer after still another quotation. "I pass from this to ask how far negation is "unreal' and 'subjective.' My book is faulty here owing to its acceptance of 'floating ideas,' and through its failure to recognize that in its own sphere every idea has reality. Discarding this error we may say at once that all negation is real, and that it is real just because it is relative. The content which it denies is never excluded absolutely. Far from falling nowhere, that content qualifies elsewhere the Universe. In this other region it owns positive truth and reality—whatever may be the amount and final character of these, and whatever the conditions under which, however much transformed, the denied content finds its goal. Unless you have a meaning and an idea (we may remind ourselves), you deny nothing; since an idea is needed for denial, and since a meaningless idea is none. And on the other side, wherever you have an idea, that idea (we have seen) has reality. And its negative relations to other things real (we further saw) belong to and qualify our Universe, even where we fail in the end to perceive how in detail this result is verified."[30]

When an idea is denied, that idea "is never excluded absolutely." But what would it mean to be excluded absolutely? It would have to mean to be apart from Reality, since Reality is that *from which* it would be absolutely excluded. Of course there is some special subject, some other idea, from which any given idea is excluded; but there is not ever *complete* exclusion of one idea from the other: they have an identity of context, both ideas being "in one with Reality." So even if one idea is excluded from another, it cannot be said to be *absolutely* excluded. And though an idea be excluded from an entire "sphere" it cannot be excluded from all "spheres." A content is absolutely excluded only if it nowhere qualifies Reality. Now the possibility of this is precisely what Bradley is denying. "Far from falling nowhere, that

---

[30] *PL,* p. 665.

content qualifies elsewhere the Universe." If no idea is utterly excluded from the Universe, or Reality, then we must accept the notion that everything conceivable is somehow real. ". . . wherever you have an idea, that idea . . . has reality."

A very strong bond between thought and Reality is established by a doctrine such as this. Reality includes everything conceivable. Now it might be argued that Bradley means that negation qualifies the real only in the sense that any negative judgment implies some positive judgment, but such an interpretation would entail both a neglect of Bradley's statement that all ideas are real and a misunderstanding of what Bradley means by judgment. Every judgment, we must remember, exhibits some one idea and that idea, whatever it is, is real. If one wants to deny any idea he must, nonetheless, express it. There must be an idea if there is to be a denial. And that idea, whether it be affirmed or denied, "has reality." Bradley is asserting, it seems, that distinctions exist in the Universe, and that negative judgments state those distinctions. In that sense, then, they qualify Reality. And any idea denied is denied of a special context, or "sphere", within the whole, not of the whole as such.

IV. There are a few considerations which might show how well this whole notion can be applied. To begin with there is the judgment in which we deny existence. If one contends: "There are no mermaids," it becomes, in Bradleian translation: "Reality is such that mermaids cannot exist." Certainly, Reality is qualified by such a statement. But the question is: in what sense can "mermaids" be said to be real? One obvious answer is that to rule mermaids out of existence is not to rule them out of Reality. Even what is relegated to limbo is real, for the realm of limbo is not excluded from Reality. Bradley would add, I suppose, that the very denial of existence to an idea presupposes an identity between that which does not exist and all that does: namely, the Reality which they share. And if there were no identity, there could be no difference; distinctions can only be made within a context.

A more difficult test, it might be thought, would be an instance in which something is denied of Reality itself. Would not that yield something which would be absolutely excluded, having nothing in common with that from which it is excluded. Of course here we must ask what could possibly be excluded from Reality. For Bradley no *idea* could ever be so excluded. All that one could exclude would be a contradiction; one might deny the name of "real" to the square circle and all its logical family. But far from being a difficult test of the applicability of Bradley's doctrine, this is no test at all. A square circle, because it is a contradiction, is not an idea at all, and the sentence in which it is excluded from Reality exhibits its meaning properly only when it is reworded so that the phrase does not occur at all.

Finally, we may raise the whole question of falsehood. If a judgment is false, how does the idea it exhibits qualify Reality? Indeed, has not the possibility of error been neglected altogether by Bradley in connection with such things as the totality of judgments, which make up the system of discourse? Would such a totality include true judgments only, and, if so, what is the justification for such a belief? In answer, a possible solution might be found to stem from the notion that every judgment exhibits but one idea. An idea is a sign, a meaning. One might go on from here to contend that a sign must be a sign *of* something. If there is nothing of which it is a sign, then there is no meaning and, properly speaking, no sign. It follows, of course, that in such a case there is no idea either. If a false judgment be one which does not correspond to the situation it purports to describe, then that judgment cannot contain an idea, since the situation *of which* the supposed idea would be a sign, does not even exist. The false judgment, then, would be one which did not contain an idea; to put it more accurately, the words under consideration would not constitute a judgment at all, since a judgment *is* the expression of some one idea. Our conclusion from this must be that, by definition, error has no place in judgment and, indeed, the phrase "false judgment" is a contradiction in terms.

The analysis above, though based on Bradley's definition of judgment, is specious in the context of his other doctrines. All ideas, he contends, have reality. And to say that a group of words does not exhibit an idea unless they correspond to some actual situation is merely to argue in a circle, for it is like saying that all ideas are real and if any so-called "idea" is not real (does not correspond to an actual situation), then it is not an idea. (This is a good example of petitio principii, if of nothing else).

An answer to the question as to the place of false judgments might be offered which would also be based on Bradley's definition of judgment, and would still be more adequate than the last. An idea is a sign, we might contend, even if that idea is false, so long as there is a conceivable (non-contradictory) situation for which it stands. Insofar as the judgment expresses an idea, it expresses Reality; but insofar as it expresses a false idea, it does not express, or qualify, existence (or whatever other realm it is within which the idea purports to hold). All ideas express Reality, all have some place within it, for Reality, we must conclude, contains all non-contradiction. An idea false in one context must be true in another.

As to the place of the false judgment within the totality of judgments: truth, understood as a matter of coherence, dominates that totality, for it is nothing if not coherent. The utterly false, as I pointed out in greater detail in discussing coherence, is distinguished by, and in a sense eliminated because of, incompatibility with the complex of true judgments, and so might be said to be not false, but meaningless, and hence no judgment at all. Still, on Bradley's account, it seems that there is a place for false judgments, which, being judgments, cannot be utterly false; a way in which they dovetail into the sum of all judgments, within which, of course, they would be recognized for what they are.[31]

V. The position Bradley held with regard to the negative judgment in the *Logic* did not really have to undergo much change to become the position adopted in the *Terminal Essays*. Apart from "floating ideas" the essentials of the argument are very much the same. But the pervasive influence of "floating ideas" had colored negation with a subjective cast, and it is that subjectivity, which had prevented Bradley from developing his final doctrine earlier, that he is here at some pains to deny. In discussing contradiction in the *Logic*, Bradley had written: "Contradiction is thus a 'subjective' process, which rests on an unnamed discrepant quality. It can not claim 'objective' reality; and since its base is undetermined, it is hopelessly involved in ambiguity. In 'A is not B' you know indeed what it is you deny, but you do not say what it is you affirm. It may be a quality in the nature of things which is incompatible with A, or again with B. Or again it may be either a general character of A itself which makes B impossible, or it may be some particular predicate C."[32]

In a note on one of his earlier statements Bradley makes quite clear the change that has taken place in his position and, indeed, the way in which that developed into a more adequate concept of Reality. The original statement was: ". . . logical negation can not be so directly related to fact as is logical assertion. We might say that, as such and in its own strict character, it is simply 'subjective:' it does not hold good outside my thinking. The reality repels the suggested alteration; but the suggestion is not any movement of the fact, nor in fact does the given subject maintain itself against the actual attack of a discrep-

---

[31] The way in which they fit can be understood with reference to what they are, for what is normally called the false is for Bradley a degree of the true.
[32] *PL,* p. 124.

ant quality. The process takes place in the unsubstantial region of ideal experiment. And the steps of that experiment are not even asserted to exist in the world outside our heads. The result remains, and is true of the real, but its truth, as we have seen, is something other than its first appearance."[33] This argument, of course, rests on the analysis of a negative judgment to mean: "Reality is such that A is not B" or "that there are no AB's." Since there are no AB's in Reality but, nevertheless, since we talk about them, all AB's must be mental. The entire meaning of this is altered by Bradley's note: " 'Fact' here should be 'perceived fact.' And negation is 'subjective' in the sense that *mere* negation, *mere* exclusion, is an abstraction and is by itself really nothing at all. Otherwise negation is *not* 'subjective', though it is *more* 'reflective' than is affirmation."[34]

By changing "fact" to "perceived fact," Bradley denies that negation is not so fundamental an expression of the Universe as is affirmation. The Reality on which all logic depends is a more sweeping and comprehensive conception in the notes and the *Terminal Essays* than it is in the *Logic*. By changing "subjective" to "reflective," Bradley is arguing that, although negation as such is no more "subjective" than is affirmation, there is a difference in the levels of reflection on which they belong: there is a greater degree of understanding entailed in comprehending the negations (and disjunctions) implied in every judgment than there is in merely grasping bald affirmations. In considering the same point in the *Terminal Essays* Bradley restates the same belief in greater detail, making clear the way in which the change in his position coincides with his changed (or more consistently developed) conception of Reality. "Hence, again, negation is not 'subjective.' You may, when it is compared with affirmation, call it, if you please, more 'reflective,' in the sense that we, perhaps generally, know that we assert, before we know that we deny. But such prior or greater awareness is irrelevant to the point here at issue. The distinctions in our 'objective' world do not become merely 'subjective', because we can be said to make them or again because we know that we make them. On the contrary they form the essential structure of that world. The attempted suggestion which our denial repels rests (we saw above) on a real identity in that which has proved incompatible; and a real difference under that identity is asserted in our rejection. Negation in short implies at its base a disjunction which is real, and its goal is to set before us reality as a systematic and explicit totality of complementary differences. To such an ideal world

[33] *PL*, p. 120f.
[34] *PL*, p. 127.

(I would repeat) we can not wholly attain, and even in principle any such world falls short of ultimate truth and reality. But on the other side our result approaches and embodies that perfect end with a fullness and actuality far beyond that gained by any mere affirmation. For the simple positive is no more than a one-sided abstraction, that, like mere 'matter of fact,' lies at the furthest remove from final reality and truth."[35]

VI. In a full understanding of the negative judgment as sketched by Bradley in the above quotation, the final touch is added to the scepticism of the author. Negation more than affirmation approximates the nature of that system which would "set before us reality as a systematic and explicit totality of complementary differences," but neither can quite attain it. And even if we could attain this goal, we should still not have attained "ultimate truth and reality." Such a position leaves us far from the ends we seek and makes even keener our doubts about the validity of the very strictures we are imposing and the analyses on which they rest. In writing of other matters Bradley uses language which should be appropriate here, and I quote one section: "If finally the reader asks as to the place assigned by metaphysics to the ideas just discussed, the answer briefly is as follows. Such reality as these ideas possess, is, in the first place, not ultimate. We must deny, that is, that, taken as they are in themselves, these ideas can be real. For their being consists in and only stands by an abstraction which breaks up, and which, if maintained, must destroy the living Reality. But the further question as to how abstraction, being such, can itself be possible, and can appear as fact—is in the end unanswerable. It is but one aspect of the ultimate enquiry as to how there can come to be such a thing as finite existence. Here, in my opinion, it is useless to seek for what is called an explanation. But, on the other hand, the question how, in the Whole and in the end, all abstract one-sidednesses are made good, can, I think, in principle be answered. Nothing in any appearance, so far as that something is in any sense positive, can conceivably be lost; and so much as this seems certain. On the other side, by addition, by resolution, and by reunion in a more concrete totality, the divisions and the conflict of appearances can everywhere be harmonized. And all one-sidednesses, thus transformed, can contribute each its full content to the unbroken and self-complete Reality."[36]

"The ideas just discussed," which are the concern of the preceding section, are those of the impossible, the unreal, the self-contradictory,

---

[35] *PL,* p. 665f.
[36] *PL,* p. 672f.

and the unmeaning. Yet, because of the character of the final judgments Bradley passes on logic, I venture to believe that if the "ideas" under consideration be taken to include the entire argument of the *Principles of Logic,* this section would still be accepted by its author. His belief that even if the whole which is best approximated by the negative judgment could ever be attained (and it cannot), we should still not have "ultimate truth and reality", leads us to the conclusion that the whole judgmental complex, were it perfect, would still be an abstraction, a portion severed from the full life of Reality. How much more, then, are individual judgments abstractions? All, indeed, would seem to be abstraction that is not itself the whole. Why the ideal world which we hold as the goal of all our logic would not, even if it were attained, be "ultimate truth and reality," is a question whose answer is not found here. Bradley refers the reader to *Appearance and Reality,*[37] where he offers a solution. In turning to that essay in metaphysics after an examination of the *Principles of Logic* and its *Terminal Essays,* one may well be aware, in advance of opening the volume, of the outline of that work, of some of the questions it must attempt to answer, and of the principles which can be used as an instrument of scepticism; and one can be sure that an application of those principles in any methodical way would force the author to reject most of the established ways of understanding the world.

---

[37] *PL,* p. 666, footnote.

CHAPTER IV
APPEARANCE

1. INTRODUCTORY

I. *Appearance and Reality* is one of those volumes which provide a rallying-point for thinkers who have a common basis of belief but who need, in their own day, something more than the books of the past to justify their cause and to gain them new adherents. There is something of the missionary in most philosophers, whether it be conscious or not. They take their places amid the strife of warring sects and strive to proselytize among their opponents and among the youth who are eager to learn and to weigh. They do not offer salvation as a goal, unless they be intellectual soldiers of some church, but rationality. "Come unto us," they invite, "and your questions shall be answered, or we shall show you that they are not questions at all." Polemic is important or is deemed so; adversaries must be refuted or it must be demonstrated that their doctrines are only a portion of the truth. Great books of the past may nourish and sustain living men in their work but new books are always necessary to deal with specific matters. Plato attacked hedonism and the final word on the subject may perhaps be found in the pages of the *Dialogues,* but new manifestations of that doctrine require new answers. Bradley himself did not merely refer the Utilitarians to Plato but rather offered his own critique of their beliefs. And every so many years a new book is necessary, a book which is systematic in character and comprehensive in scope, a book which offers, like those of the philosophers who have greatest reputation among us, a complete orientation, culminating in one specific attitude, toward the problems of philosophy. That is the kind of book that Bradley gave to his generation when he wrote *Appearance and Reality*.

Edward Caird, when Bradley's book was published, decided that it was the greatest thing of its kind since Kant; Hastings Rashdall, writing later and adding a faint note of caution to high praise, said that there had been nothing greater since Kant. *Appearance and Reality,* indeed, answered all the specifications. It was comprehensive enough and systematic enough (and, of course, closely reasoned throughout) to be accepted as a great book, if, that is, it spoke (as it did) for a strong enough group or represented an important tradition. The lack of explicit polemic (Bradley commented: "I have . . . abstained from historical criticism and direct polemics"[1]) was no deterrent since, in the first place, a strong, systematic argument can easily take the place of polemic, and, in the second place, *Appearance and Reality* in fact contains a great deal of polemic. The paradoxes of Zeno contain no mention of the men at whom they were aimed but one may be sure that the Pythagoreans of his day knew, without being named, that they were among them. So readers of Bradley may easily recognize, although there is no explicit reference to them, the thinkers whose doctrines are confuted.

The chief philosophical tradition of the England of Bradley's youth was that of British Empiricism, with its early and somewhat muddled beginning in Francis Bacon and its maturity in a succession of thinkers from Locke to John Stuart Mill. As German philosophy found more and more acceptance across the channel, a vigorous attack was launched on empiricism under the leadership of Thomas Hill Green, who was followed by men like Caird and Nettleship, Bradley himself, Bosanquet, and Haldane. The new English idealism was developed in polemic and reached its height, perhaps, in Bradley's carefully contrived system. As Professor Brand Blanshard puts it: "Empiricism was . . . a very versatile theory, appearing in logic as psychologism, in metaphysics as skepticism, in ethics as hedonism."[2] Bradley's chief works, he thinks, are attacks on the various aspects of this one philosophy: the *Logic* refutes psychologism; *Appearance and Reality* destroys the pretensions of scepticism by the construction of an Absolute; and the *Ethical Studies* strikes viciously at hedonism.

As I understand Bradley's procedure, he employed a double-edged weapon; he used a criterion, developed by his studies in logical theory, as a sceptical instrument which could destroy the chief categories of his opponents' philosophy; then, turning the criterion around, he constructed a positive doctrine of his own. But the sceptical edge of the criterion cut into his own construction, and he was constrained to point out the limitations of man's knowledge of the very Reality on which he insisted. Then, coming under the fire of the young realist and pragmatist movements of England and America, he wrote the papers published as *Essays on Truth and Reality*, in order, among other things, to show his critics that, within sharply defined limits, he could accept many of their doctrines.

As for the tradition in which the earlier book was written, it is, of

---

[1] *AR*, p.x.
[2] *Journal of Philosophy*, vol. XXII, p. 11.

course, the great tradition of Absolute Idealism. For British Idealists, who relied for a treatment of central problems on the Germans, *Appearance and Reality* was evidence that their philosophy had really taken root and flowered at home. Rashdall wrote of Bradley's significance that ". . . to me one great value of Mr. Bradley's teaching consists in this—that he is the most thoroughly convinced and the most convincing, I venture to think the most irrefutable, of Idealists."[3] Idealist theses are, of course, argued, and, in the main, accepted by Bradley; but he was not (no important philosopher has ever been) merely an echo of his tradition, or the tradition become incarnate. The question, even, of just what doctrines constitute a tradition is always a moot one. Bradley's metaphysical doctrines were based, for good or ill, on his system of logic, a system not without roots in the past but one, certainly, that was, in many respects, highly original.

II. The logical conclusions to which Bradley had been led provided him with an instrument both of scepticism and construction, an instrument that he used to yield both denial and belief. On the first page of the *Introduction to Appearance and Reality,* the way in which the doctrines of his *Logic* are woven into his metaphysical argument is interestingly exemplified. He writes: "The man who is ready to prove that metaphysical knowledge is wholly impossible has no right here to any answer. He must be referred for conviction to the body of this treatise. And he can hardly refuse to go there, since he himself has, perhaps unknowingly, entered the arena. He is a brother metaphysician with a rival theory of first principles. And this is so plain that I must excuse myself from dwelling on the point. To say the reality is such that our knowledge cannot reach it, is a claim to know reality; to urge that our knowledge is of a kind which must fail to transcend appearance, itself implies that transcendence. For, if we had no idea of a beyond, we should assuredly not know how to talk about failure or success. And the test, by which we distinguish them, must obviously be some acquaintance with the nature of the goal. Nay, the would-be sceptic, who presses on us the contradictions of our thoughts, himself asserts dogmatically. For these contradictions might be ultimate and absolute truth, if the nature of the reality were not known to be otherwise."

The essentials of Bradley's rejoinder to his supposed critic are, as he points out, "plain," in that many thinkers have taken a similar attitude. But the actual statement is based on the kind of analysis to which his logical doctrines entitle him. "To say the reality is such that

---

[3] *Proceedings of the British Academy,* 1911-1912.

our knowledge cannot reach it, is a claim to know reality." But who made such assertion about reality? The imaginary critic? That gentleman is simply "ready to prove that metaphysical knowledge is wholly impossible." It seems that a distinction might be made between those who enter the field of metaphysics to prove the point and those who do not. But Bradley makes no such distinction. Indeed, he does not even ask in what such proof would consist. He writes as though all who condemn metaphysics are thereby implicitly asserting a proposition in metaphysics; and on his analysis of the judgment, that is the case. He has so defined judgment that all assertions and denials, no matter what their immediate context, are ultimately to be regarded as in the realm of metaphysics. The phrase, "metaphysical knowledge is wholly impossible," is to be understood, in the light of the *Logic,* as meaning "the reality is such that our knowledge cannot reach it." And, as a result, all who doubt the possibility of metaphysical truth are "brother metaphysicians" who may only prove their point by entering the lists and tilting against their opponents. And without any chance of success, for they are already committed to a view of reality implicit in their own words. This is by no means Bradley's only use, in the construction of his metaphysical argument, of reality as the subject of all judgment; the transition from appearance to reality, crucial to the entire structure of the book, would go to pieces without it.

Certain of the dicta which Bradley urges in making his points about appearance do not have the cloak of logical sanction in which the difficulties of the above argument are hidden. Typical of these other statements is a contention which is made more than once in Bradley's pages and which is a not unfamiliar error in the history of thought, Bishop Berkeley being, perhaps, one of the offenders. In arguing against the reality of space or extension as a primary quality or qualities, Bradley writes: "But there is a more obvious argument against the sole reality of spatial qualities; and, if I were writing for the people an attack upon materialism, I should rest great weight on this point. Without secondary quality extension is not conceivable, and no one can bring it, as existing, before his mind if he keeps it quite pure."[4] Underlying this statement is the assumption that the conceivable is always a kind of mental image, like a picture, a notion which entails, as a consequence, the belief that all our ideas must be of this sort, if they are to have any validity. The attack on the distinction between primary and secondary qualities, familiar since Berkeley, has often suffered from the use of this principle, which so

---

[4] *AR,* p. 13f.

many users, Bradley among them, have been glad to forget or deny, as they proceeded with their work.[5]

III. The crux of Bradley's treatment of appearance, the argument which is basic to its acceptance, is that concerned with relation and quality. The criterion on the basis of which Bradley distinguishes between appearance and reality, the principle of non-contradiction, is used in such a way that the contradictory is classified as appearance and the non-contradictory as reality. The world may be thought of in terms of relation and quality, primary and secondary qualities, substantive and adjective, space and time, motion and change, causation, etc. If these can be shown to be self-contradictory concepts they may be regarded as appearance. Examination of them can proceed by means of analyses calculated to reveal inconsistencies, and the examinations must be made on the basis of what is to be understood by the terms employed. Here the *Logic* stands Bradley in good stead. He is enabled, by formulating the meaning of propositions in terms of principles enunciated in the *Logic,* to discover contradictions in what might otherwise stand up under analysis. (An example of this is found in his answer to the man who denies the possibility of metaphysical knowledge.) It might seem that in this kind of procedure the matter of relations and qualities would bear no more and no less weight than that of space and time, or any of the others. But this is not the case. All the categories in terms of which we understand the world, the categories of mind, the windows through which we see all things, and the categories of things themselves, are all intelligible only in the light of relations and qualities (if qualities are taken as synonymous with terms), for it is only by the use of relations and qualities that we think at all. For this reason Bradley, in his logical writings, having despaired of the attainment of truth by means of relational thinking, had to give up the hope of attaining truth by thinking.

One might expect that Bradley's condemnation of relations and qualities would be closely connected with the doctrines of the *Logic*. But if so, how would Bradley's own doctrine differ from that of the sceptic whose denial of the possibility of metaphysical knowledge had been dealt with so firmly? And if Bradley persisted in believing metaphysical knowledge possible, would he not have to champion a method for attaining truth other than that of rational thinking? In that case the *Logic* could be seen in perspective as a work whose purpose in the system of its author's thought was the discovery of the lim-

---

[5] See *AR,* p. 144. Bradley comments: "The common view, which identifies image and idea, is fundamentally in error."

its of reason in order to pave the way for the exaltation of some other avenue to knowledge—intuition, perhaps, or faith. And one might conclude that, in outline at least, Bradley was closer to Kant than he was to Hegel. A strange theme this would be in the history of scepticism and dogma; a rejection of rational thinking coupled with a belief in man's ability to attain truth in metaphysics; a theme nonetheless strange for having been heard before.

The aseptic sweep of Bradley's dialectic is itself an element in the puzzle. What is the value of all his analysis and of his attempts to convict of self-contradiction, if rational thinking cannot yield truth? Or is it, perhaps, that the "law of contradiction" has some warrant denied to relational thinking as such? If so, is that marvellous principle even statable completely apart from relations? These are questions that require answering if one is to understand *Appearance and Reality,* but for the answers one must look to the whole system therein expounded.

2. RELATION AND QUALITY

I. The chapter entitled *Relation and Quality,* which is the third in the book, is, explicitly, that on which the entire section called *Appearance* depends. Bradley starts the chapter thus: "It must have become evident that the problem, discussed in the last chapter (substantive and adjective), really turns on the respective natures of quality and relation."[6] And the final paragraph states: "The reader who has followed and has grasped the principle of this chapter, will have little need to spend his time upon those which succeed it. He will have seen that our experience, where relational, is not true; and he will have condemned, almost without a hearing, the great mass of phenomena."[7] What he sets out to prove he states succinctly: "The arrangement of given facts into relations and qualities may be necessary in practice, but it is theoretically unintelligible. The reality, so characterized, is not true reality, but is appearance."

II. Appearance, we see, is reality, but it is not true reality. And "the arrangement of given facts into relations and qualities" is appearance. The whole notion is at first difficult to grasp. The arrangement into relations and qualities is not thought of as part of the order of reality but rather as an operation of mind or an order that is thought. This is evident from Bradley's statement that such arrangement "may be necessary in practice, but it is theoretically unintelligible." Such a comment could not have been intended to refer to

---
[6] *AR,* p. 21.
[7] *AR,* p. 29.

reality. The difficulty lies in calling this arrangement "appearance", something that is reality but not true reality. The chief question here, it seems to me, is what it is that Bradley is calling appearance. It may be "an order that is thought" or it may be "that such an order is thought." The distinction I am trying to express may perhaps be more clearly stated in other words. Since men think of "given facts" in terms of an order of relations and qualities, Bradley may relegate to the category of appearance this order which they think or the fact of their thinking it in such a manner. The latter is a "fact" in the sense of being an event in space and time. As such, in what sense could it be called appearance? In the obvious one, perhaps, since it appears as an event. But why would such an event not be true reality? The order which is thought, on the other hand, does not *appear* in the same sense, nor in the common sense of being present to bodily sensation. It does, however, exist, in any sense in which thoughts, whether true or false, may be said to exist. So we might say it is reality and if it is a falsification of nature,[8] there might be meaning in distinguishing it from "true reality." The existence of an arrangement of facts into relations and qualities would not be of the same kind as an existence of an order of nature; its existence would be that existence which is appropriate to falsehood. And Bradley's distinction between such an order, as appearance, and "true reality," strengthens such an interpretation. For the opposite of "true reality" is "false reality."

Bradley, then, is referring to all thought which is characterized by arrangement of elements into relations and qualities, and this he classifies as appearance, which so far seems to be tantamount to falsehood. Just what is meant by including it under the heading of reality, whether it is thought of as a kind of experience which falsifies Reality, or as some realm of "subsistence," or merely as some of the things men have thought when they were in error, is a question we must pursue later. It is interesting to note, however, that if the latter course is taken, what may seem at first to be merely an attitude of "common sense" may quickly come to be a reassertion of the doctrine of floating ideas; for floating ideas are just those in which content is severed from existence, ideas which err. And it was in the course of such an attempt to pursue "common sense" that the doctrine of floating ideas was first formulated.

III. The discussion of relation and quality commences with the contention that "qualities are nothing without relation."[9] One can

---
[8] I use the word "nature" in its ordinary sense rather than in the special meaning with which Bradley invests it.
[9] *AR,* p. 21.

never find qualities without relations; identity and difference, at least, are relations fundamental to the consideration of any quality. And if we try to isolate qualities by a process of abstraction, the process itself implies relations. It is possible to contend that the product is independent of the process which gave it birth but such a position is, in the end, indefensible. Product must always be thought of in terms of the process whose end it is. Any attempt to separate the two is self-defeating because "any separateness implies separation, and so relation."[10]

If qualities are meaningless considered apart from relations they are in no better case when taken together with them. This is the basic attack on the arrangement into quality and relation, this and the contention that the position of relations with respect to qualities is also unintelligible. Qualities cannot be reduced to relations alone, for "relations must depend upon terms, just as much as terms upon relations."[11] Here Bradley embarks upon the familiar argument that, since qualities must be what they are and also must be in relation, i.e. must be made, somewhat, what they are by the relations in which they are placed, the whole notion exhibits a contradictory character which leads, ultimately, to infinite regression. The crux of the analysis, perhaps, can be found in the following: "But how the relation can stand to the qualities is, on the other side, unintelligible. If it is nothing to the qualities, then they are not related at all; and, if so, as we saw, they have ceased to be qualities, and their relation is a nonentity. But if it is to be something to them, then clearly we now shall require a *new* connecting relation. For the relation hardly can be the mere adjective of one or both of its terms; or, at least, as such it seems indefensible. And, being something itself, if it does not itself bear a relation to the terms, in what intelligible way will it succeed in being anything to them? But here again we are hurried off into the eddy of a hopeless process, since we are forced to go on finding new relations without end. The links are united by a link, and this bond of union is a link which also has two ends; and these require each a fresh link to connect them with the old. The problem is to find how the relation can stand to its qualities; and this problem is insoluble. If you take the connexion as a solid thing, you have got to show, and you cannot show, how the other solids are joined to it. And, if you take it as a kind of medium or unsubstantial atmosphere, it is a connexion no longer. You find, in this case, that the whole question of the relation of the qualities (for they certainly in some way *are* re-

---

[10] *AR*, p. 24.
[11] *AR*, p. 26.

lated) arises now outside it, in precisely the same form as before. The original relation, in short, has become a nonentity, but, in becoming this, it has removed no element of the problem."[12]

It is difficult, with so good an illustration as this before us, to refrain from condemning most of Bradley's problems in *Appearance and Reality* as purely verbal; but, although a good case might be made for such a criticism, it would scarcely be relevant to my purpose to elaborate it. Considering the above quotation from the standpoint of Bradley's meaning and his expression of it, with reference to the *Logic,* is quite a different matter. The argument itself can, I think, be summarized as follows: (1) Either relations are in some way connected with the qualities between which they are said to hold, or they are not (and it is a contradiction to assert both). (2) If relations are not connected with qualities, our terms are self-refuting and hence nonsense, for qualities, then, would not be qualities *of* anything, and relations would not relate. (3) If relations are connected with qualities, then either the relations are merely adjectives of the terms, or else entities in their own right. (a) They cannot be considered as adjectives, because "the relation is not the adjective of one term, for, if so, it does not relate, nor for the same reason is it the adjective of each term taken apart, for then again there is no relation between them. Nor is the relation their common property, for then what keeps them apart? They are now not two terms at all, because not separate."[13] (b) If relations are connected with qualities and are entities in their own right, in what does such connection consist? Between entities such as these, connection can be effected only by means of relations, so a new relation must be postulated which would hold between the original relations and terms. And this new relation can only be understood in its connection with the other terms and relations by means of still another relation which would link all the elements involved, and so on, ad infinitum. (4) In conclusion; it is not meaningful to assert either that relations are connected with qualities, or that they are not; and since, when we talk of relations and qualities, we must think of them either as connected or unconnected, the whole relation-quality pattern of thought must be indicted and condemned.

IV. Bradley does not himself use the phrase "in connection with," which I have employed in an attempt to give his meaning, though he does write of a "connecting relation;" he asks how a relation "can stand to" its qualities, how it can succeed in "being anything" to them. The use of either type of phrase reveals, some would say, the

---
[12] *AR*, p. 27f.
[13] *AR*, p. 27, footnote.

ultimate meaninglessness of Bradley's problem, as it stands, for the connection under consideration seems to be that of relation, and the question that of the relation between a relation and its terms. Indeed, Bradley makes this explicit enough, when he writes: "But if it (a relation) is to be something to them (terms), then clearly we now shall require a *new* connecting relation." And if a relation be conceived as the way in which terms *stand to* each other (and that seems Bradley's use of the word), surely it is meaningless to ask how "the way in which terms stand to each other" itself stands to the terms.

At the time Bradley asks the question, however, he is assuming that a relation is like a term in "being something itself," for the only alternative he has offered is that of being a "mere adjective," an alternative quickly rejected as "indefensible," for reasons quoted. So that Bradley is only urging the necessity of an infinite regression as a principle of explanation *if we assume* that relations are entities of the same type as terms. And so stated there is little quarrel to find with Bradley's position. Unfortunately the position is often misstated so that it is thought to be the contention that the notion of arrangement into relations and qualities itself entails an infinite series of relations to make it intelligible. And this misunderstanding is sometimes the basis on which Bradley's argument is adjudged false or meaningless.

V. The chief difficulty in understanding Bradley's position on the question of relations and qualities lies, I think, in something else, which can perhaps be made explicit by examination of the passages I have already quoted. "The arrangement of given facts into relations and qualities . . . is theoretically unintelligible." Two things may be meant by such an arrangement: (1) the habit of perceiving the world as a pattern of qualities and relations, or (2) the habit of describing the world in such terms. The first is really the contention that the world (or the system of existence) is experienced as an arrangement of facts in the form of relations and qualities; the second is the contention that discourse consists in placing "given facts," which may or may not themselves be experienced as within such an arrangement, within a pattern of terms and relations. Bradley adds to the sentence just quoted: "The reality, so characterized, is not true reality, but is appearance." This may be taken to mean that "the arrangement of given facts into relations and qualities" is an experienced order or one thought to be such, which, insofar as it is experience, is within reality but which does not hold of the ultimate structure of the real. And such an interpretation would be consonant with the ordinary meaning of appearance. On the other hand, the proposition under consideration may be interpreted as asserting that "the arrangement of given facts into relations and qualities" is an order of discourse which, insofar as it is discourse, is within reality but which, insofar as it is false, does not hold of the ultimate structure of the real. Thus what I originally characterized as "an order that is thought" is seen as having two possible senses: (1) it is an experienced order which is thought to be the order of Reality, but which, nonetheless, is not; (2) it is an order *of thought* as well as one that is thought, being the order that is fundamental to discourse, but it, nonetheless, falsifies Reality.

It may be thought that the meaning which eventually can be assigned to "appearance" will determine which of the above interpretations is to be put on "the arrangement of given facts into relations and qualities," for, whereas the traditional meaning of appearance as experience which falls short of reality is in consonance with the first interpretation, the meaning I suggested before, that of falsehood, seems more in consonance with the second. Bradley's use of "term" and "quality" as synonyms, however, makes it seem that both interpretations are to be accepted. The order of experience, then, is the order of thought. We think erroneously when we attribute to Reality the actual order in which we experience phenomena and in terms of which we explain them. Let me quote once more, at this point, the beginning of the section on the connection of relations and qualities. "But how the relation can stand to the qualities is, on the other side, unintelligible. If it is nothing to the qualities, then they are not related at all; and, if so, as we saw, they have ceased to be qualities, and their relation is a nonentity. But if it is to be something to them, then clearly we now shall require a *new* connecting relation. For the relation hardly can be the mere adjective of one or both of its terms; or, at least, as such it seems indefensible. And, being something itself, if it does not itself bear a relation to the terms, in what intelligible way will it succeed in being anything to them?" This exhibits a clear shift from qualities to terms without, apparently, any intention to alter the meaning. But such a transition utterly confuses the question as to whether the propositions in this chapter are intended to hold of experience or of discourse unless we accept them as holding of both.

VI. To substantiate the interpretation of "appearance" as both discourse and ordinary experience, and to raise a question about truth, there is at least one more sentence of Bradley's in this section which should be considered. I quoted, to begin with, the way in which Bradley closed the chapter on *Relation and Quality*. One of the sentences reads: "He (the reader) will have seen that our experience, where relational, is not true; and he will have condemned, almost without a hearing, the great mass of phenomena." Certainly it would seem, on the basis of this statement, that the relational order which is attacked throughout is an order of experience. It still may be proper to refer to it as an order that is thought but only if it be realized that it is thought because it is experienced. Where Bradley says that "experience, where relational, is not true," he raises a question as to the meaning of truth, more detailed consideration of which must be postponed. But at least it may be noted that there seems to be the assumption that it is legitimate to predicate truth and falsity of experience itself. The qualifying phrase, "where relational," may be taken to distinguish experience of one kind from experience of another kind; relational experience is false, some other kind, perhaps, is true.

Truth implies a criterion of the true; and it may be that what Bradley means, taking the structure of the real as criterion, is that a certain kind of experience falsifies reality. The falsifying experience, which is relational, must include "the great mass of phenomena," for that is condemned as soon as one realizes that relational experience is not true. If one attempts to determine precisely what is included in this mass of phenomena, perusal of the section on *Appearance* can yield the answer. All the phenomena therein condemned, as Bradley explicitly asserted, are condemned because they are relational in structure. And they constitute virtually the whole realm of phenomena, a realm which men have tried to make intelligible on the basis of relation and quality.

There is, indeed, nothing of importance in the realm of phenomena that is omitted from Bradley's list. And yet a little reflection shows that there is at least one strong discord in this logical symphony of condemnation. Bradley's language is highly inappropriate as a description of his subject matter. "The great mass of phenomena" should be condemned by the reader "almost without a hearing;" and having grasped the principle underlying the criticism of relation and quality one scarcely needs to follow the explicit application of that principle to the "phenomena" with which Bradley finds it desirable to deal. All this he tells the reader; yet if the reader list the "phenomena" he is supposed to be ready to condemn, he can hardly refrain from saying that they are not phenomena at all. Primary and secondary qualities, substantive and adjective, space and time, motion and change, causation, activity, things, self,—these pass in the catalogue for categories. They are the ways in which men have tried to explain phenomena. And it is difficult to resist the conclusion that Bradley is not condemning *phenomena* to the realm of appearance; rather he is condemning *traditional categories* in terms of which men have tried to render phenomena intelligible. If, however, these categories are not only ways of understanding the world, but also ways in which that world is experienced, then Bradley is condemning both phenomena and our manner of interpreting them. What is essential to his argument is what is made clear in trying to fix the meaning of "phenomena." Bradley is attacking certain traditional ways of thinking about the world which are based upon normal experience and he is denying that such experience is ever experience of Reality. It is in this way that he is characterizing as "appearance" the categories which provide him with chapter headings in Book One and the experience which is subsumed under those categories.

VII. Turning now once more to the section already quoted, which I called the crucial argument in the chapter on *Relation and Quality,* there are several difficulties in what purports to be a dialectical demonstration, which are noticeable at once. A consideration of two of these should show the need for an analysis based on the *Logic.* To begin with, there is the implied metaphor of the chain, which is a strange linguistic figure for the connection of terms by relations. "The links are united by a link," he writes, "and this bond of union is a link which also has two ends; and these require each a fresh link to connect them with the old." Now, the very nature of a chain is such that each link is itself interwoven with the next, and any two links connected by one which is between them will each be locked around the connecting link. Certainly the link in the middle will have two ends, but each end will be laced about the link which is nearest. It is absurd in the extreme to suppose that each link which furnishes the connection between two others will require still additional links before it can be united with them. The reason I have addressed myself first to this analogy is that the purpose of figures of speech, apart from any aesthetic values they may possess as ornament is, fundamentally, illumination. A figure may, and often does, in the hands of a great writer, function as a searching beam of light into what had been hitherto dark and obscure. Yet this figure simply serves to emphasize the reader's first puzzled objection to Bradley's whole argument: that it is not really a question to ask how, or by what, relations are connected to the terms between which they are said to hold, for the very meaning of a relation is that it is such a connection between terms.

VIII. There is in the argument, also, an ambiguity which results in an apparent incomplete disjunction, sapping the force of the ultimate contention. The relation, he has said, cannot be "nothing to the qualities," for then it would not, in any intelligible sense, be a relation. On the other hand, "if it is to be something to them," then "the relation can hardly be the mere adjective of one or both of its terms; or, at least, as such it seems indefensible. And, being something itself, if it does not itself bear a relation to the terms, in what intelligible way will it succeed in being anything to them?" As I understand this, Bradley is contending that, if the relation actually provides a connection between terms ("if it is to be something to them"), then it must be either an attribute of terms ("the mere adjective of one or both of its terms") or an actual entity, itself substantial ("being something itself"). The former alternative being "indefensible," we must accept the latter. But the latter requires an additional relation between relation and terms to explain it and so is no more acceptable than the former.

To say that the relation must be regarded as either substantive or adjective (conceptions which Bradley had just finished attacking), even were it justifiable, would not be sufficient to make Bradley's point. There would still be necessary the narrow way in which he uses the idea of "substantive," a word which he did not actually employ in this context. The phrase he used: "being something itself," is fundamentally ambiguous, for it is supposed to connote only the contradictory of "mere adjective." That which is not a "mere adjective" may be regarded as an entity of some kind and it might be legitimate to say that it must be "something itself;" but it is not legitimate to assume that the only kind of entity is one which is on the same level as qualities. Yet that is Bradley's assumption, an assumption necessary for the remainder of the argument. Without it the question as to the manner in which the relation can "stand to" its qualities is quite meaningless. And with it Bradley's disjunction seems incomplete. The reader can simply refuse to accept either of the alternants offered, contending that to be "something" does not mean necessarily to be something of any given type, and that relations, though "something," are quite different in function from qualities, being by nature that which provides connection between them.

IX. I have introduced this examination of a point basic to Bradley's argument about relations and qualities in order to show that, considered apart from the doctrines of the *Logic,* and from Bradley's enterprise as a whole, the entire discussion is ambiguous and untenable. Our question now is: in terms of the *Logic,* how may Bradley's argument be understood?

X. All thinking, Bradley had asserted, is incurably relational, and as a result is forever barred from comprehending reality. Yet he had not in detail examined the notion of relation and quality which must act as a fundamental category in thinking about anything whatever. If that basic notion itself could be shown to be self-contradictory it should then be possible to use its very meaninglessness as an argument against all other categories which depended upon it in any way. Another way of getting the same results (a way Bradley employed) would be to discover the precise way in which relations and qualities were self-refuting concepts and then to show that all the ways of understanding that were based on them exhibited the same fundamental flaw.

How, we must ask, can the notion of relational connection (assuming that Bradley makes no distinction between relation in discourse and connection in experience) be proven contradictory in terms of the doctrine of the *Logic?* It is easy enough to argue that all judgments hold of reality and that, since all judgments assert relation and there is no relation in reality, judgments, and hence relational thinking (or, simply, thinking, since "relational thinking" is redundant), is erroneous. But among other difficulties with such an argument, it is question-begging: reality is understood as non-relational because the concept of relation is self-contradictory. Before proceeding to a more careful construction it might be advisable to quote from the first chapter of the *Logic* a short section showing the original set-up of judgment and relation in Bradley's thought. "We take an ideal content, a complex totality of qualities and relations, and we then introduce divisions and distinctions, and we call these products separate ideas with relations between them. And this is quite unobjectionable. But what is objectionable is our then proceeding to deny that the whole before our mind is a single idea; and it involves a serious error in principle. The relations between the ideas are themselves ideal. They are not the psychical relations of mental facts. They do not exist between the symbols, but hold in the symbolized. They are part of the meaning and not of the existence. And the whole in which they subsist is ideal, and so one idea."[14]

Here, it seems, Bradley distinguishes sharply between meaning and existence, and insists that relations are part of the former only. But in the light of his total view it is more fruitful to emphasize that when Bradley writes that relations are "part of the meaning," he means that they "hold in the symbolized," which is "one idea." Relations and terms, then, constitute a whole, a single idea, which in judgment is predicated, as a whole, of reality. And, as I have tried to show, the recognition of the two-fold nature of the subject simply

---

[14] *PL*, p. 11.

refined, but did not discard, this fundamental point. To think of judgment in this way is to think of relations as integral portions, along with what are called terms or qualities, of a single apprehended context, discriminations within which are no doubt useful but, nonetheless, irrelevant to the unity of the context.[15] The alternative to this view, according to Bradley, would be the notion that a judgment contained two really separate terms and that, under certain conditions and in certain respects, these are united by a relation separate from, or external to, them.[16]

This alternative position is, presumably, a statement of the ordinarily received doctrine of judgment. The very denial that a judgment consists, fundamentally, in one idea which is predicated of reality (or, as he put it later, in the exhibition of reality under two aspects: selected and ultimate), implies the belief that a judgment consists of atomic elements which are, in the judgment, synthesized for the moment. These elements would have to be the terms and relations which make up the judgment; the terms being substantial entities and the relations being either substantial or insubstantial (and, if insubstantial, "mere adjective"). But the relations are elements in the judgment, not merely adjectives descriptive of the terms. As such they must be of the same general type as the other elements, the terms. The disjunction between adjective and substance rigidly conceived is thus made complete. In this context in which relations are not thought of as intrinsic to a single exhibited whole, they must be elements in some sense external to the terms between which they are said to hold and, being external, they must be more than the actual connectedness of those terms. How then, the question arises, can the terms be related, since being related consists in being elements within some larger context? In a judgment understood in this manner there is no whole within which the elements exhibit the unity, or "togetherness," which is necessary to their being related; there are, on the contrary, separate elements, terms and relations, which are not, actually, related at all. And to try to relate them by the addition of another relation is to raise the same question, and so on, endlessly.

On the other hand, suppose Bradley's own analysis of judgment (which is the contradictory of the analysis just considered) be offered as an explanation of the difficulties of relation and quality. We find it to be no more adequate. The elements which compose any whole are so intimately connected with each other and with the whole (as, for example, the qualities of an apple are connected with each

---

[15] *PL*, pp. 11-13, 49.
[16] *PL*, pp. 287-292.

other and with the apple) that there is no connection of the type of relation at all. (How is the redness of an apple related to the texture of the skin?) Yet discourse consists in abstracting the elements from a total situation and placing them in relations of one sort or another. And in doing this the contradictions already considered are at once made manifest. Even if we refuse to analyze some whole, the question of its connection to some other whole will intrude the notion of relation. The only alternative is to try to experience immediately any total situation and to refuse to analyze, or to classify it at all. But this is no longer thinking and, if the contradictions of quality and relation are not found on the level of such experience, they are found in thought and in the normal experience of mankind, an experience always mediated by the constructs of intelligence.

XI. In the *Logic,* Bradley has been concerned chiefly with the totality which he thought was implied by any consideration of the individual, and with the position, within that totality, of the individual as it was cognized in terms of idea, judgment, and inference. In Book One of *Appearance and Reality* he focused his attention on the individual in itself in order to show that only the ultimate whole was consistent. Considered as a part of reality, the individual was, as we have seen, always somewhat true and real and, on the other hand, always somewhat false and unreal (unreal only in the sense of not being fully reality). It is in this sense that appearance is reality, but not true reality.

When the individual is considered in itself, however, it is simply inconsistent, and any theory which does not recognize the Absolute, which is all-embracing reality, is a theory committed to the defense of doctrines which are contradictory. Even the concrete universal, although providing a better way of explaining mediated experience than by independent terms and relations, is, inasmuch as it falls short of the ultimate whole, beset by the same problems of relation as the alternative doctrine; the difficulties are merely less apparent. "A being, short of the Whole, but existing within it, is essentially related to that which is not-itself. Its inmost being is, and must be, infected by the external. Within its content there are relations which do not terminate inside. And it is clear that, in such a case, the ideal and the real can never be at one. But their disunion is precisely what we mean by imperfection. And thus incompleteness and unrest, and unsatisfied ideality, are the lot of the finite. There is nothing which, to speak properly, is individual or perfect, except only the Absolute."[17]

---

[17] *AR,* p. 217.

The ideal world and experience containing mental constructs are thus to some extent one, for the ideal world is that which is the recognition of such experience in thought. When Bradley writes of the separation of the 'what' from the 'that', this distinction between the ideal and the real is what is intended. For the ideal to lose its imperfection it would have to be more than 'what'; it would have to be Reality. Though such a consummation be devoutly wished it is impossible of fulfillment. Reality can never be known because the nature of thought is such that it is forever a stranger to the utterly inclusive, consistent, and non-relational totality.

CHAPTER V

APPEARANCE AND REALITY

1. THE CRITERION (I)

I. Bradley's extensive use of a criterion of reality raises certain problems which cannot, unfortunately, be treated together, since a full understanding of the criterion is dependent upon a knowledge of its place in the "levels of reality." I propose, therefore, to consider first whether or not the criterion is really a criterion at all, that is, whether it is a methodological principle which can aid investigation, or whether it is only a description, virtually definitive, of reality. I shall contend that it is the latter and, in a later place, shall try to justify the contention further, in terms of Bradley's scepticism.

II. Any discussion of the meaning of "appearance" for Bradley must be also a discussion of the meaning of "reality," for the two are like opposite sides of the same coin; one is, to use the traditional language of logic, the full contrapositive of the other. When he comes to the subject of *The General Nature of Reality*, Bradley writes: "Is there an absolute criterion? This question, to my mind, is answered by a second question: How otherwise should we be able to say anything at all about appearance? For through the last Book, the reader will remember, we were for the most part criticizing. We were judging phenomena and were condemning them, and throughout we proceeded as if the self-contradictory could not be real. But this was surely to have and to apply an absolute criterion. For consider: you can scarcely propose to be quite passive when presented with statements about reality. You can hardly take the position of admitting any and every nonsense to be truth, truth absolute and entire, at least so far as you know. For, if you think at all so as to discriminate between truth and falsehood, you will find that you cannot accept open self-contradiction. Hence to think is to judge, and to judge is to criticize, and to criticize is to use a criterion of reality. And surely to doubt this would be mere blindness or confused self-deception. But, if so, it is clear that, in rejecting the inconsistent as appearance, we are applying a positive knowledge of the ultimate nature of things. Ultimate reality is such that it does not contradict itself; here is an absolute criterion. And it is proved absolute by the fact that, either in endeavoring to deny it, or even in attempting to doubt it, we tacitly assume its validity."[1]

The assumptions throughout this paragraph are obvious enough. In order to adjudge anything true or false we need a criterion, not of *truth*, but of *reality*. This shift in ground is even more evident here than in the last section. Bradley is no longer talking only about the truth or falsehood of judgments, but about the truth or falsehood of phenomena as well. And even insofar as he thought of the "phenomena" as categories (which they seem to be) there is still a shift: categories are not judgments and cannot be said to be true or false in the same sense. Calling a phenomenon true would seem to be identical with calling it real, just as calling it false would be identical with calling it appearance. An absolute criterion, he insists, is one whose validity is a necessary assumption even when it is being denied or doubted;[2] it is what we might call a necessary proposition. Here we may recall that the possibility of metaphysical knowledge is, for Bradley, absolute in the same sense.

The argument itself is simple: we constantly condemn the inconsistent, hence we must accept the consistent. Again there is the question as to how all this can refer to phenomena. Can a phenomenon be inconsistent? Or consistent, for that matter? But if Bradley is really dealing with the views about phenomena implied in the use of certain categories, he is concerned with what he would call judgments, and so with the ways in which phenomena enter discourse. In any event, the form of the argument is more clearly stated by Bradley in another place, where he writes: "If we can be sure that the inconsistent is unreal, we must, logically, be just as sure that the reality is consistent."[3]

III. As I said before, the propositions are contrapositives of each other, the criterion of reality being simply an immediate inference from that of appearance. The criterion of appearance may be derived from the actual procedures of analyzing its content, procedures to be found in the section on appearance in Bradley's book. The content, then, of appearance, has been made known and its structure analyzed. But what of the content of reality? That has not yet been considered since an understanding of it is dependent on just this criterion of consistency or non-contradiction. How then can we know, at this point in the argument, that the concept of reality has any denotation at all? Certainly not on the basis of the inference which yielded its criterion.

---

[1] *AR*, p. 120.
[2] *AR*, p. 120.
[3] *AR*, p. 123.

Bradley's insistence in the *Logic* that all universal categorical judgments are to be understood as hypothetical can be taken as precluding that possibility. Neither "the inconsistent" nor "the reality" is guaranteed existence by the judgments in which they occur. But the "inconsistent" has as ostensive reference, among other things, substantive and adjective, space and time, causation, etc. Still we cannot argue from this that reality is more than an empty concept or, in other language, a null class. That reality is more than this, that it is a concept with exemplification, can be accepted only on the basis of its necessity as a background of all thought; more specifically, that there is something which is designated by the term "reality," is an implication of all judgment and so of thought itself. I think it is on this ground that Bradley accepts the denotation of reality. And the argument implicit in such acceptance is by no means free from difficulty.

The objections may be listed under two headings. In the first place, the systematic whole which Bradley insists is the necessary condition of judgment and inference need not be reality at all; it might with just as great plausibility be contended that it is the system of discourse. Not that any predication would be made of discourse in the same sense in which Bradley asserts that it is made of reality; but that the idea S-P, which is the content of a judgment, could be regarded, by some solipsist for example, as having warrant only by virtue of its position in the entire structure of his thought. This is an objection which is, perhaps, too unimportant to expand. But the second objection is more vital. To argue that there *is* reality because reality is implicit in all judgment, somehow smacks of the ontological argument. It is dubious on more than one count. First, the existence of discourse is not sufficient warrant for the conclusion that whatever is essential to its structure must be contained in the world which it considers. It might, for example be basic to the language or the categories employed. And perhaps only insofar as discourse is a portion of existence is existence qualified by the nature of discourse. Secondly, it might be contended that what is meant by "reality" which is implicit in all judgment is something which must, by its very nature, exist. This, of course, is the traditional form of the ontological argument[4] and is subject to all the criticisms that have been made of that device. I shall not attempt to add to all that has been written about the subject save to comment that I should be prepared to admit that the ontological argument is the only *demonstration* of existence

---

[4] Explicitly Bradley disavows the ontological argument thus: ". . . the ontological argument cannot prove the existence of practical perfection." (*AR*, p. 132.)

that I know, just as value is the only reason that I know to explain *why* a thing exists, but both seem unacceptable and the questions which give rise to them belong, I think, to the regions of theology and myth rather than to those of philosophic enquiry.

IV. As a systematic consideration it is interesting to ask how the statements: "the inconsistent is unreal" and "the reality is consistent" would be transformed on Bradley's account of the proper way to interpret all judgments. There is not much difficulty with the first. "Reality is such that the inconsistent is unreal," is probably an adequate statement. But, remembering the distinction between true reality and what is presumably false reality, the above proposition could not be understood to mean "reality is such that it does not (or can not) contain the inconsistent." Reality does *contain* the inconsistent, as Bradley reminds the reader more than once; but the inconsistent is not reality and reality is not inconsistent. Considered as a portion of reality, the inconsistent loses its character and somehow merges into a consistent totality.

The second statement has a strange ring when put into this form. "Reality is such that the reality is consistent," probably should be taken to mean only "reality is such that it is consistent." The nature of reality consists fundamentally in being consistent. But, remembering that appearance, or the inconsistent, is in reality, although it is not true reality, we may wonder whether "reality" does not have a different meaning in each of its uses in our transformed proposition. In its first use it might mean the totality of the whole and in its second "true reality" as distinguished from appearance. On the other hand, such a totality is probably what is meant by "true reality." No matter how the issue is decided, there can be no question that reality itself is, for Bradley, the whole, and that it is thoroughly consistent.

This consistent character of reality is for Bradley an Ariadne-thread which may be followed through the labyrinthine problems of the Absolute. And only by following it can the intellectual adventurer come to his journey's end. It is a principle from which all knowledge of the Absolute can be deduced. As I shall try to show, the full meaning of consistency for Bradley is the Absolute, and the full meaning of inconsistency is appearance. The terms should really be reversed. Appearance is defined as the inconsistent, which is another name for the incomplete; the Absolute is defined as the consistent, which is another name for the Whole. And, though inconsistency is a sceptical criterion, for one can discover contradictions, consistency turns out to be no criterion at all.

V. The importance of this "criterion" in Bradley's scheme is sufficient warrant for considering it a bit more closely. As Bradley treats it, the assertion that the reality is consistent is itself a positive criterion which is the logical result of the negative, "the inconsistent is unreal." Bradley's actual argument is based on his contention in the *Logic* that all denial implies affirmation. He states the objection and meets it thus: "But it may be said that this ('ultimate reality is such that it does not contradict itself') supplies us with no real information. If we think, then certainly we are not allowed to be inconsistent, and it is admitted that this test is unconditional and absolute. But it will be urged that, for knowledge about any matter, we require something more than a bare negation. The ultimate reality (we are agreed) does not permit self-contradiction, but a prohibition or an absence (we shall be told) by itself does not amount to positive knowledge. The denial of inconsistency, therefore, does not predicate any positive quality. But such an objection is untenable. It may go so far as to assert that a bare denial is possible, that we may reject a predicate though we stand on no positive basis, and though there is nothing special which serves to reject. This error has been refuted in my *Principles of Logic*."[5]

Obviously, if the assertion of consistency means only the denial of inconsistency, the only change from a negative to a positive criterion has been one of form, or statement. So Bradley must show that there is something more involved in the concept of consistency than the mere denial of contradiction. "The question is solely as to the meaning to be given to consistency. We have now seen that it is not the bare exclusion of discord, for that is merely our abstraction, and is otherwise nothing. And our result so far is this. Reality is known to possess a positive character, but this character is at present determined only as that which excludes contradiction.

"But we may make a further advance. We saw . . . that all appearance must belong to reality. For what appears is, and whatever is cannot fall outside the real. And we may now combine this result with the conclusion just reached. We may say that everything, which appears, is somehow real in such a way as to be self-consistent. The character of the real is to possess everything phenomenal in a harmonious form.

"I will repeat the same truth in other words. Reality is one in this sense that it has a positive nature exclusive of discord, a nature which must hold throughout everything that is to be real. Its diversity can

---

[5] *AR*, pp. 121-122.

be diverse only so far as not to clash, and what seems otherwise anywhere cannot be real. . . . Appearance must belong to reality, and it must therefore be concordant and other than it seems . . . the real is individual. It is one in the sense that its positive character embraces all differences in an inclusive harmony. And this knowledge, poor as it may be, is certainly more than bare negation or simple ignorance. So far as it goes it gives us positive news about absolute reality."[6]

When we add to our criterion the knowledge that appearance is within reality, this excerpt informs us, we possess considerable information about the structure of reality; but even without it the criterion of reality is positive. The use of the word "positive" is, I submit, something less than lucid. It is, in itself, a protean adjective, whose usage in any specific context should have its dimensions made explicit. Certainly Bradley's emphasis on the "positive" nature of the criterion shows that he attaches great importance to the term in this connection. If we ask precisely what it means for a criterion to be positive, rather than negative, the answer, I presume, would be in terms of the function of the criterion. A positive criterion, it would seem, is a criterion which may be employed in the business of discovery; anything conformable to it could be said to be a member of the class of which it is the criterion. A negative criterion, on the other hand, would be one which would have a purely eliminative function; anything *not* conformable to it would be barred from membership in the class of which it is said to be the criterion.

In the section last quoted, Bradley uses the word "positive" in a way that should permit us to determine whether or not the above suggestion as to the meaning of positive and negative criteria is at least compatible with his. He writes: "Reality is known to possess a positive character, but this character is at present determined only as that which excludes contradiction." Reality is not merely that which excludes contradiction; it is something with an actual structure, about which, at the moment, all that is known is that it is thoroughly consistent. The "positive character" of reality would seem to be its actual structure. But in order to learn that structure the criterion of the real, already arrived at, must be employed. And the "positive character" of the criterion must consist, also, in something else. That can only be, it seems to me, the manner of its employment. And in this respect the criterion is negative; for it is not a criterion of discovery but rather one of elimination. In order to be positive, as

---

[6] *AR,* p. 123f.

I have defined the term, the criterion would have to be fully convertible; from "the reality is consistent" one would have to be able to infer: "the consistent is real." This can be done only when the statement is construed as definitive of one or the other of its terms and, in that case, "consistent" will mean an all-encompassing harmony, valid enough in Bradley's metaphysic but methodologically valueless.

As a description of reality in Bradley's terms, "the consistent is real" should be a supplement to "the reality is consistent," if the term "consistent" be taken as "ultimately consistent," i.e., as consistent with an infinite body of knowledge. Anything which is consistent is this sense would be real, for it would be a portion of the total structure of reality. Taken as a methodological principle, however, "the consistent is real" has no such warrant. One cannot discover what is ultimately consistent; it is a sufficiently difficult task to discover what is consistent within some field or sub-field. Consistency in this sense (and this alone is ultimate for those who do not think of the world as one gigantic system) is all that can be considered methodologically. But if something can be found to be consistent within some small field, i.e., consistent with all else in that field, it cannot therefore be said to be real, for it cannot therefore be said to be "ultimately consistent," which I take to be the meaning of Bradley's criterion.[7]

Insofar as method is concerned it seems, then, that the word "consistent" would have to be construed in its "special" rather than its "ultimate" sense. And, so construed, the assertion that "the reality is consistent" is convertible only by limitation. "The consistent is real," its full converse, would follow only if subject and predicate had the same meaning, so that we would again mean "ultimately consistent." By the same token, the full converse is legitimate where the propositions are taken as descriptions of reality, for the "ultimately consistent" is a definition of the real. As a methodological principle, "the real is consistent," can have only the negative function of eliminating from reality all that, in the special sense, can be shown to be inconsistent. This principle, we may conclude, has no methodological advantage over its contrapositive, "the inconsistent is unreal."

VI. There is one more modification that should be made before we take our leave, for the moment, of Bradley's criterion. Even that which can be shown to be inconsistent in the special sense (that which

---

[7] Of course, it might be objected that the consistent, in any sense, is real, for reality includes it, as it does all else. But then, everything is included in reality and the criterion of reality would be no criterion at all, but a final description of its structure.

is inconsistent when offered as ultimate explanation), is not to be barred from total reality, for it is to be classified as appearance, or false reality, which is itself a portion of the real. The entire doctrine might be thought to make little sense if the self-contradictory were to be included, although some among the New Realists might at one time have thought that legitimate. But, unless it be false to think of the *Logic* as a system which excludes the meaningless, the self-contradictory could not, as expression, ever be regarded as a judgment, for it could have no meaning and, in experience, it could not be said to exist, since it has no content.[8] We must postpone further consideration of the criterion until we have treated the doctrine of "levels of reality."

2. LEVELS OF REALITY

I. Appearance can best be understood in terms of its position in the total scheme of Bradley's metaphysic. It is best to consider it, therefore, together with immediate experience and the absolute. I shall be concerned in the section which follows with two chief themes and with the introduction of a third. I shall treat (1) experience as the content of reality; (2) the levels of reality; and (3) I shall commence a discussion of satisfaction as the criterion of truth. The question concerning appearance with which we were left at the close of the last section was: How can appearance, which is not true reality, be said to be contained within that reality?

II. At this point there is raised with added force the question of the significance of the distinction between false reality and any other kind, the question, in short, of the meaning of "appearance," which, being within reality, must be understood if we are to understand reality. In response to a question as to the content of the individual and systematic Absolute (a word synonymous with reality),[9] Bradley writes: "When we ask as to the matter which fills up the empty outline, we can reply in one word, that this matter is experience. And experience means something much the same as given and present fact. We perceive, on reflection, that to be real, or even barely to exist, must be to fall within sentience. Sentient experience, in

---

[8] See *AR*, pp. 128-129.

[9] It is interesting to note that "reality" is capitalized throughout the *Logic* and uncapitalized throughout most of *Appearance and Reality*. In the latter volume, however, the Absolute always appears with an initial capital. It is perhaps an idle speculation that the Absolute was sometimes regarded by Bradley as "true reality," the system of the whole, whereas "reality" was then taken to mean anything within that whole, so that appearance was reality, though it was not the Absolute.

short, is reality, and what is not this is not real. We may say, in other words, that there is no being or fact outside of that which is commonly called psychical existence. Feeling, thought, and volition (any groups under which we class psychical phenomena) are all the material of existence, and there is no other material, actual or even possible. This result in its general form seems evident at once: and, however serious a step we now seem to have taken, there would be no advantage at this point in discussing it at length. . . . I will state the case briefly thus. Find any piece of existence, take up anything that any one could possibly call a fact, or could in any sense assert to have being, and then judge if it does not consist in sentient experience. Try to discover any sense in which you can still continue to speak of it, when all perception and feeling have been removed; or point out any fragment of its matter, any aspect of its being, which is not derived from and is not still relative to this whole. When the experiment is made strictly, I can myself conceive of nothing else than the experienced."[10]

It is important to note that experience is not contrasted with thought but rather is said to contain it. It is interesting, too, to note the three traditional categories Bradley calls to mind: feeling, thought, and volition, for they become a portion of the total pattern that he weaves.

III. Within the total context of experience so understood, Bradley distinguishes the level of thought in some detail. "I will try to state briefly the main essence of thought, and to justify its distinction from actual existence. It is only by misunderstanding that we find difficulty in taking thought to be something less than reality.

"If we take up anything considered real, no matter what it is, we find in it two aspects. There are always two things we can say about it; and, if we cannot say both, we have not got reality. There is a 'what' and a 'that', an existence and a content, and the two are inseparable. That anything should be, and should yet be nothing in particular, or that a quality should not qualify and give a character to anything, is obviously impossible. If we try to get the 'that' by itself, we do not get it, for either we have it qualified, or else we fail utterly. If we try to get the 'what' by itself, we find at once that it is not all. It points to something beyond, and cannot exist by itself and as a bare adjective. Neither of these aspects, if you isolate it, can be taken as real, or indeed in that case is itself any longer. They are distinguishable only and are not divisible.

---

[10] *AR*, p. 127f.

"And yet thought seems essentially to consist in their division. For thought is clearly, to some extent at least, ideal. Without an idea there is no thinking, and an idea implies the separation of content from existence. It is a 'what' which, so far as it is a mere idea, clearly *is* not, and if it also *were*, could, so far, not be called ideal. For ideality lies in the disjoining of quality from being."[11]

The level of thought is the level of appearance. Both are defined in the same manner. "Now appearance is content not at one with its existence, a 'what' loosened from its 'that'."[12] It seems obvious that this whole notion may be a consequence of the doctrine of "floating ideas,"[13] but I think the same notion could have appeared, though in perhaps slightly different language, on the basis of Bradley's logical approach as a whole. Actually, I think, Bradley is committed to it by the section on appearance and would have had to arrive at it whether or not he included any mention of "floating ideas." Thought, he insists, is everywhere relational and the relational involves contradiction. The level of relation and quality is the level of thought and, with or without "floating ideas" this level is equated with appearance.

As has already been pointed out, the 'what' and the 'that' are regarded as separate in the *Terminal Essays,* long after Bradley's disavowal of "floating ideas." Their separation is the separation of the ideal and the real (when the latter is taken as the Absolute). As we shall see later, when Bradley says that an idea is real, he does not mean that it is completely any real individual. The qualities of an individual which constitute an idea of it are not the complete individual. What is left out is, perhaps, the inherence of that individual in the Absolute. The individual as a portion of the real is not identical with the individual considered in itself; their difference is the difference of the real and the ideal. The former is both existence and content and the latter only content (since the existence or reality of the individual consists in its place in the Whole). And the ideal content can never be completely true because the true content of an individual depends on its existence, that is, it depends, ultimately, on its place within the Absolute.

IV. The distinction between false and true reality is further complicated by a distinction between false and true appearance. "Error is the same as false appearance, or (if the reader objects to this) it is at any rate one kind of false appearance." Since appearance is false reality, false reality must be of two kinds: false false reality and true

---

[11] *AR,* p. 143f.
[12] *AR,* p. 165.
[13] See, for example, the treatment of judgment, *AR,* p. 144ff.

false reality. "Appearance then will be the looseness of character from being, the distinction of immediate oneness into two sides, a 'that' and a 'what'. And this looseness tends further to harden into fracture and into the separation of two sundered existences. Appearance will be truth when a content, made alien to its own being, is related to some fact which accepts its qualification. The true idea is appearance in respect of its own being as fact and event, but is reality in connection with other being which it qualifies. Error, on the other hand, is content made loose from its own reality, and related to a reality with which it is discrepant. It is the rejection of an idea by existence which is not the existence of the idea as made loose. It is the repulse by a substantive of a liberated adjective. Thus it is an appearance which not only appears, but is false. It is in other words the collision of a mere idea with reality."[14]

The word "appears," in the penultimate sentence, seems crucial. In what sense do appearances appear? Since appearance is the level on which there is thought and since appearance contains thought, the answer seems to be: in the sense of experience which can be thought. And it must be noted that such experience is itself mediated by thought. It is as if Bradley were saying that, though in thought there is not the potency necessary for the comprehension of reality, one still has to distinguish between true thought and false thought. Here I must again appeal to the notion of special and ultimate, basic terms for the understanding of this metaphysical system. All discourse is ultimately false in that it is incapable of revealing reality; but in a restricted, or special sense, discourse may be either true or false. The way in which, in the *Logic,* the special subject develops only insofar as it is a portion of the residual, or ultimate, subject is an analogue of the way in which any object is real only insofar as it is a portion of the Absolute. (Here Bradley is closer to the development of the doctrine of the twofold nature of the subject as it is found in the *Terminal Essays* than he is to the original statement of it in the first edition of the *Logic.*) "In the end no finite predicate or subject can possibly be harmonious."[15] Thought is capable of revealing the nature and connections of finite objects insofar as they are finite. It is only "in the end" that they are inconsistent, that is, in contrast to the ultimate. Insofar as we employ thought to deal with them in their "selected" sense, we employ a medium that may yield relatively valid results.

The absurdity of the language of which we have been making use

---
[14] *AR,* p. 166.
[15] *AR,* p. 167, footnote 1.

(true false reality, appearance appearing) does not affect Bradley's conclusions. The realm of appearance is, as originally suggested, the realm of falsehood, but only in the ultimate sense of being incapable of describing reality. Within the field of the ultimately false, of appearance or false reality, we may have either truth or falsehood in the special, or selected, sense of an adequate or inadequate description of the finite as finite.

"There will be no truth which is entirely true, just as there will be no error which is totally false. With all alike, if taken strictly, it will be a question of amount, and will be a matter of more or less. Our thoughts certainly, for some purposes, may be taken as wholly false, or again as quite accurate; but truth and error, measured by the Absolute, must each be subject always to degree."[16] The purposes for which our thoughts may be taken as entirely true or false are those which, I take it, arise on the level of appearance. Yet even these are but true and false in some degree when thought of in terms of the Absolute.

The degree of truth to be assigned to any judgment may be determined by the application of two criteria: internal harmony and all-inclusiveness.[17] In the end, (a phrase as common in Bradley as "in the long run" is in the writings of so many economists), both criteria may be seen as aspects of a single principle. "The truth and the fact, which, to be converted into the Absolute, would require less rearrangement and addition, is more real and truer. To possess more the character of reality, and to contain within oneself a greater amount of the real, are two expressions for the same thing."[18] The system of perfectly true judgments and the totality which is the Absolute are one and the same. If one could attain (what is impossible) the complete harmony of a consistent series of judgments he would be in possession of an all-embracing system of knowledge, for all sub-systems are inconsistent unless related to all other sub-systems and, ultimately, to the whole. If this is all that Bradley means, it is simply another of the consequences of his definitions of judgment and inference, a consequence already evident in the *Logic*. But the notion that truth and reality are actually the same is also contained in Bradley's words. This is a belief not entailed by his original definitions and seems rather to be a return to those sections in the *Logic*, on which we have already commented, in which truth was identified with, not a description of existence, but existence itself. Not unknown

---

[16] *AR*, p. 320f.
[17] *AR*, p. 321f.
[18] *AR*, p. 323.

in the history of philosophy, this doctrine seems to take on overtones in Bradley's statement of it which are not common to all who have uttered the doctrine before. Could some intelligence become omniscient it would have done more than completely comprehend reality; it would have merged with the Absolute, become indissolubly one with it. The sounding of such a mystical note seems possible only on the basis of the previous identification of existence with experience, for then detailed comprehension of the whole would not be understanding of an independent existence, as in a Realistic philosophy, but the attainment of a harmonious, all-inclusive experience, which is itself the Absolute. Indeed, in terms of the conclusions already reached by Bradley, an ultimate mysticism seems almost inescapable.

V. The experiential matrix which is the content of reality is the third of the levels of reality, not insofar as it is separated from the others, for it contains them, but rather as the totality which is intended by the self-transcending character of each of the others. The first of the levels is less inclusive than the second but, in a sense, more harmonious; the second is both less inclusive and less harmonious than the third. In another sense the first level is the least harmonious as well as the least inclusive of the three. "Experience in its early form, as a centre of immediate feeling, is not yet either self or not-self. It qualifies the Reality, which of course is present within it; and its own finite content indissolubly connects it with the total universe. But for itself—if it could be for itself—this finite centre would be the world. Then through its own imperfection such first experience is broken up. Its unity gives way before inner unrest and outer impact in one. And then self and Ego, on one side, are produced by this development, and, on the other side, appear other selves and the world and God."[19]

Immediate feeling-experience, the first level of experience, actually contains both self and not-self, characteristics of the second or relational level. But these are as yet not distinguished. They are simply a portion of an undifferentiated manifold, a stage of experience prior to reflection, and are submerged, as are all relations, in the depths of child-like experience. Of course the word "child-like" is an inadequate adjective as a description of such experience. This entire stage is a fiction as monstrous as the social contract, an abstraction from the realm of relations and qualities in which thought recognizes its natural habitat. But it is not the level of thought at all; it is the level of pure feeling. And pure feeling is only the mythical given,

---

[19] *AR*, p. 465. See also pp. 229, 265, 417, 464.

the datum, in a new dress. Bradley knows quite well that thought, feeling and will are all involved in experience and he is simply characterizing as best his terms permit the materials on which thought operates.

Immediate experience is less inclusive than relational experience in that the distinctions within it are unrealized. It is more harmonious in that the contradictions arising from those distinctions are as little realized as the distinctions themselves. But it is less harmonious in that more rearrangements and adjustments must take place before those inconsistencies can disappear: rearrangements which include the initial sharpening of the discrepancies by the attainment of the relational level. The very instability of immediate experience which is due to the unrealized distinctions within it aids in bringing about relational experience. That is to say, pure feeling disappears as distinctions are made; but sensuous experience persists as the basis of relational experience. The world at the level of relations still contains the underlying feeling-manifold in which it had its origin. So that, although the sensuous given is transcended, it is not transcended by movement to a different context. Its transcendence remains within the context of experience.[20]

Relational experience, which is the level of thought based upon feeling, is no less unstable. Permeated by contradiction, it points to a totality which is a unity in diversity and within which all contradiction is simply discrimination within a total context, a completely harmonious and all-inclusive whole. Judgment, basic to this level of reflective experience, contains within itself a constant reference to something beyond the level of the "special subject," an "ultimate subject" which is reality. Again transcendence takes place within the context of experience. Reality contains all appearance, which is reflective or mediated experience based on the sensuously given, and holds it in a higher unity than the undifferentiated manifold of the immediately given.

VI. The intellect is driven from stage to stage because it can never be satisfied with anything inharmonious or incomplete.[21] Although thought may never attain its proper end in the Absolute, yet it is

---

[20] See *AR*, p. 465f.

[21] One may be tempted to qualify the substantive "intellect" by the adjective "Bradley's." The temptation is increased by a passage such as the following: "I could not rest tranquilly in a truth if I were compelled to regard it as hateful. While unable, that is, to deny it, I should, rightly or wrongly, insist that the inquiry was not yet closed . . . if the main tendencies of our nature do not reach consummation in the Absolute, we cannot believe that we have attained to perfection and truth." *AR*, p. 130.

ever describing the whole in some manner, for all predication has reality as ultimate subject. Like some mariner doomed to wander always far from home, thought finds its consolation in considering the general features of that to which it can never win. The very notion that reality is implied by the character of judgment, a doctrine stated in the *Logic* and taking on new colors from the subtle dyes of *Appearance and Reality,* may be regarded as an enormously complex manner of begging the question of the validity of the ontological argument. The specific question as to whether the essence of anything can imply its existence is begged by the thesis that the basic element of thought, the judgment, implies the existence of everything that actually does exist, and implies further that all things constitute a whole.

Bradley seems to psychologize this thesis by writing: "Thinking is the attempt to satisfy a special impulse, and the attempt implies an assumption about reality. You may avoid the assumption so far as you decline to think, but, if you sit down to the game, there is only one way of playing. In order to think at all you must subject yourself to a standard which implies an absolute knowledge of reality; and while you doubt this, you accept it, and obey while you rebel."[22] There are, one may suppose, generic characters of rationality to which one must submit himself if he is to participate in any communicable inquiry. But, in the light of the thesis that metaphysics must yield what is satisfactory to the intellect, Bradley's words may mean more than this simple statement. After all, any investigation must make use of fundamental categories of explanation and, in this respect, metaphysics is in no different condition from any other discipline. Bradley means, as our last footnote shows, that metaphysics must end in some harmonious view of the whole in which all the chief pyschological wants of mankind can find their satisfaction. The argument perhaps can be summarized, by an unkind critic, in this fashion: there is a psychological necessity to attain to harmony in our beliefs about the universe; therefore the universe is harmonious. Stated so baldly an injustice is probably done Bradley by the absence of the glowing colors in the rich palette of his prose. But essentially it seems to contain a doctrine he accepts. And, so stated, it is simply a first order enthymeme, the implied major premise of which would be the general proposition: all psychological necessities of belief are predicates true of the universe. This, I submit, constitutes, on Bradley's part, an extraordinarily frank statement of the dialectic underlying all uses of the ontological argument, not excepting his own.[23]

---

[22] *AR,* p. 134f.

[23] One might point out further that, despite Bradley's hatred of hedonism, this constitutes a hedonist thesis that the Utilitarians never attempted to propose.

On the other hand, it is not easy to tell whether this aspect of Bradley's thought provides the motivation for the intimate relation between man and the world in which he lives, which is so important a doctrine in his philosophy, or whether it is a consequence of that doctrine. When we return to this desire for the realization of fundamental aspirations, in a place where it can be better understood,[24] it will be seen to be a far more profound and subtle theory than it seems in the description of it above.

VII. Since immediate experience is chiefly characterized as the domain of feeling and appearance as the domain of thought, it would be aesthetically proper for reality to be the domain of will. And an argument can be made for such a triad. Reality, like truth, is that which satisfies the intellect. Why not conclude that the realization of will is the distinguishing character of the Absolute? One answer is that, since reality is not a level within the whole but an all-including Universe, that would be to give undue prominence to one element contained within it. Bradley is quite explicit in making this point. "Generally I agree that the real is what satisfies, and that no other definition of reality in the end is so ultimate as this. But in psychology I certainly cannot say that what satisfies is or has been willed. And even outside psychology I cannot take reality as being merely, or even in the first place, a satisfied will. I am unable, that is, to regard will, either in myself or in the universe, as being more than one partial aspect of the whole."[25]

3. THE CRITERION (II)

I. The principle of non-contradiction as the criterion of the real is so central to the metaphysical structure of *Appearance and Reality* that it is perhaps excusable to devote more space to a consideration of it. In addition to attempting to fix the precise meanings of contradiction and non-contradiction I shall try here to answer the question: How is it that Bradley, having discarded relational experience as an avenue to truth, can accept the principle of non-contradiction as the criterion of reality itself?

II. Immediate experience, we have learned, is a totality which includes no distinction between subject and object and within which there are no relations. Yet it is from this fundamental state that all distinctions emerge. It is attention to details within the whole that gives rise to relations and, as we start to cognize the directly felt,

---

[24] It will be treated in the chapter entitled *The Ideal and the Real*.
[25] *C.E.*, p. 594.

we become conscious of an "uneasiness" which, on anlysis, shows itself as contradiction. "Contradiction in the proper sense is made only by reflection. It is when diversities are referred to and located in the same point that they clash. When we analyse (and to think we must analyse), the immediate bond of union with its unknown condition, is perforce more or less discarded. The diversities can hence no longer come to us as somehow conjoined. And, attempting to connect them simply, thought forces them into an open conflict, where our felt uneasiness is developed before us into explicit contradiction."[26]

Having started to analyze, we have shattered the whole in which diversities existed without clashing, the ground on which they rested, the actual manner of their union. Nor can it be recaptured, for it was only a state of feeling and so not susceptible of being analyzed without being destroyed. The attempt to reconcile diverse elements is now committed to a pursuit of the conditions which would render contradiction meaningless, by including inconsistent elements in the thoroughgoing harmony which is the Absolute. Until they are seen as portions of reality (and they never can be) these elements remain, although contradictory, more or less true, for their contradiction consists in incompleteness, in not having within themselves the conditions which would render them consistent. Contradiction is, indeed, merely a lack of completeness, and so an inharmoniousness, for only the whole is thoroughly consistent. Contradiction is, in a word, appearance. "Contradiction in the proper sense thus belongs to the middle space of our reflective world, and it may be said to inhabit that region, or rather part of that region, which lies between feeling and perfect experience. But contradiction is perceived nowhere except on the ground of a neutral conjunction, present to sense or imagination, and it is possible only because in the end it rests and is based on felt positive experience. And contradiction, we may add, is erroneous only because it is deficient, because the condition on which the contraries were conjoined is in part suppressed, and because the condition of their higher unity has not been supplied. We should, however, remind ourselves that this problem, like other problems, is but soluble in part. The immediate immanence of the one reality in finite centres has always to be presupposed; and this fact, we have seen from the first, remains inexplicable."[27]

---

[26] *TR*, p. 270.
[27] *TR*, p. 271f. The first sentence of this section shows that, although it has been maintained that Bradley did not believe in the perfection of the Absolute at the time he wrote the essays which make up this book, he had not in fact given up that doctrine. The phrase, "higher unity" which occurs a little farther, shows that the doctrine of levels is maintained. But "higher unity" stands for nothing

III. Contradiction cannot exist at the level of immediate experience nor at that of the Absolute; it "belongs to the middle space of our reflective world." This middle space, appearance, is incomplete and therefore inconsistent. That, in a sense, is the lesson of the first book of *Appearance and Reality,* which is an attempt to exhibit the contradictions which can be discovered by an analysis of the incomplete which goes far enough. The words "far enough" would here be question-begging save that they may be taken as meaning "in the light of the whole." That, as I understand it, is Bradley's contention: the realm of appearance may be taken as containing simple contradictions and simple consistencies; but, when it is taken as ultimate, or when it is regarded from the standpoint of the whole within which it is included, it is compact of contradiction. So that the notion of contradiction, as Bradley chiefly employs it, and as it is used in the sections above quoted, may be regarded as a product of the standpoint which views appearance from the level of reality.[28]

IV. In the *Logic* contradiction is dealt with in a more traditional manner. That is, perhaps, because it is included within the system of discourse which is later seen to yield appearance. It is by reflection *on* this system, rather than by reflection *within* it, that contradiction in its fuller sense can be understood. Logic for Bradley, it must not be forgotten, is a theory of judgment and inference. Idea, judgment and inference constitute a system whose perfection would make it identical with reality, which must itself, then, comprise a system. Truth is unattainable within the system but reflection upon that system can show us, at least, in what truth would consist: namely, fulfillment of the conditions for a complete system. These conditions must consist in the way in which parts hang together to make a whole, and that we may call coherence or non-contradiction.

We know two things about a system such as Bradley is considering: (1) the parts, taken in themselves, are incomplete (this is contradiction, when viewed from the standpoint of the whole); and (2) the system, taken as a whole, is characterized by coherence and all-inclusiveness (these are not two criteria but aspects of one and may be said to constitute non-contradiction). On the basis of this knowledge we may deduce certain other propositions, such as that the whole

---

above apppearance, in the sense of *beyond* it; it means throughout something more inclusive. I think the important point is not that Bradley later gave up the "arid" intellectualism of *Appearance and Reality* for a more experiential philosophy, but rather that there was no such "intellectualism" in the earlier book.

[28] This standpoint will be treated in the chapter on *Three Theories of Truth.*

is One, a single individual. Add to this the belief that reality is made up entirely of experience and you have the reason that Bradley constantly refers to the Absolute as a single experience. These are the general characters of reality and they are arrived at by reflection upon the system of inference. But we can know no more about reality than what has just been stated. This is the scepticism to which Bradley's theory of judgment and inference commits him. The reason for it is that what we know about reality is derived from a consideration of the system of knowledge from the outside; but it is impossible, from the inside, ever to attain reality, i.e., it is impossible to complete the system. Thus it is impossible to have a detailed knowledge of the real. What we know is what it means to be reality and, further, what sort of thing is its content. And these are just the characteristics which can never be reached from inside the system.

Since we can have knowledge *about* reality (its general character) but can never know reality (its actual structure), it follows that the criterion of the real is not really a criterion (if I may be pardoned what seems a pun); it is the general character of reality and is all we can know about it. That reality consists of experience is no additional knowledge, since reality is the Whole and must contain all that is. If experience is a name for all being, the reality is experience. The only advantage gained in using such a word is the implication that there are selves and that everything conccivable must, in some sense, be present to them. That the Absolute can never be so present means, perhaps, that the true structure of the real can only be grasped in a single, all-encompassing experience and that the nature of the selves (that there are more than one is, in terms of Bradley's philosophy, only a probable inference) is such that they cannot have experiences which are more than partial.

There is, of course, a paradox in this account. All thinking is relational, and so incomplete, and we would seem to be consigned, in our intellectual efforts, to remain inside appearance, world without end. But to know anything at all about the nature of the real we must be able to view appearance, as it were, from the outside, from a standpoint which is not itself appearance. The answer that I think Bradley makes is that appearance implies its own transcendence; incomplete judgments imply, by their very nature, the complete system which contains all their conditions. Appearance, in a word, implies reality, just as the admission that we cannot know the whole implies that there is a whole which we cannot know. And the knowledge of what it would mean for appearance to be transcended, for judgment to be completed, constitutes knowledge of what Bradley calls "the general nature of reality." This much and only this much we can know. Whether or not this be deemed a satisfactory answer it is, I think, the only answer that Bradley would give and, I presume, the validity of all his statements about the Absolute is dependent upon it.

CHAPTER VI

THREE THEORIES OF TRUTH

1. POINTS OF VIEW AND THEORIES OF TRUTH

I. Bradley's work is subject to much misinterpretation on the subject of truth; at one time or another he writes from the standpoint of every major theory. The difficulty in knowing precisely what he believes is due, I think, not to any lack of clarity in the thinking but rather to what may be regarded as ambiguity in the exposition. It was perhaps this ambiguity, more than any other single factor, that necessitated the comprehensive answers to critics in the *Essays on Truth and Reality*. Bradley assumed that his readers would recognize the different points of view involved in *Appearance and Reality* and he never bothered to tell just what they were. In the Appendix which he included in the second edition of *Appearance and Reality,* published in 1897, he was already struggling with a deluge of criticism. In answer to one attack, he wrote: "I have in my book used language which certainly contradicts itself, unless the reader perceives that *there is more than one point of view*. And I assumed that the reader would do this, and I cannot doubt that very often he has done so, and I think that even always he might have done so, if he would but carry into metaphysics all the ideas with which he is acquainted outside, and not an arbitrary selection from them."[1]

It will be remembered that *The Principles of Logic* contained three different theories of truth: (1) the correspondence theory, (2) the identity theory, and (3) the coherence theory. The first two were explicit and the third, for the most part, implicit. I shall try to show that Bradley retained all three theories by making certain distinctions in context, and shall try to show, further, what those distinctions were and in what manner they affected Bradley's views about truth.

I have already pointed out that the language of all three theories occurs in *Appearance and Reality;* it remains to explicate the points of view in terms of which they are justifiable. If one considers Bradley's doctrine of the levels of reality it is at once obvious that any one accepting the doctrine could write from the point of view of one rather than another or could shift from one to the other. Bradley was constantly shifting, usually without explicit recognition of what he

---

[1] p. 496. Italics mine.

was doing. One cannot very well survey anything from the standpoint of immediate experience, for that is a non-reflective level in which thought does not exist. From the standpoint of appearance, however, it is possible to view all three levels; and from the vantage point of reality it is possible to do the same. It may be objected that reality cannot be known and so cannot be used for any such purpose; one cannot look at the countryside from the top of a hill, as one cannot look at the top itself, if it is impossible to scale the hill. The answer is that, although reality cannot be known in all its richness, it is quite possible, on Bradley's doctrine, to learn the general characteristics which it exhibits. And these characteristics Bradley has explicitly stated.

No theory of truth can be formulated which could hold of immediate experience for there is, at that level, no thought. There is, further, little excuse for attempting to formulate a theory about reality as seen from the standpoint of appearance, for the general nature of reality is known and so provides us with the most adequate point of view for surveying the whole, which is itself. On the other hand, man, in all his more practical pursuits, has need of a criterion which will not pretend to be ultimate, and, in metaphysics, desires to evaluate his daily judgments in terms of the Absolute. Thus, for truth, there are three points of view: (1) that of appearance from the standpoint of appearance; (2) that of appearance from the standpoint of reality; and (3) that of reality from the standpoint of reality. The first of these has as criterion of truth, correspondence; the second has coherence; and the third, identity.

Although all these theories have a place in *Appearance and Reality*, only the coherence theory is treated at any length, being the subject of the twenty-fourth chapter. This emphasis is in perfect accord with the chief points of view of the book: that of appearance from the standpoint of reality and that of reality from the standpoint of reality, the former being stressed with regard to truth. The lack of emphasis on appearance surveying itself led many readers to the conviction that it was not even considered. Bradley's answer came in the *Essays,* in which he restated his position on appearance from the point of view of itself and developed, in some detail, its consequences. This new emphasis is, perhaps, responsible for the belief of some critics that Bradley radically modified his earlier metaphysical doctrines when he came to write the *Essays*.[2] To me, however, it seems clear that the *Essays* contains an elaboration of a point of view with which he had not been so concerned heretofore, but the essentials of which had

---

[2] For example, Rudolf Kagey, in *The Growth of F. H. Bradley's Logic.*

been stated. Bradley's attitude towards other doctrines is stated in a section of *Appearance and Reality* in which he is looking on the work of his brain and finding it good. "Outside our main result," he writes, "there is nothing except the wholly unmeaning, or else something which on scrutiny is seen really not to fall outside. Thus the supposed Other will, in short, turn out to be actually the same; or it will contain elements included within our view of the Absolute, but elements dislocated and so distorted into erroneous appearance. And the dislocation itself will find a place within the limits of our system."[3] The actual treatment accorded his critics follows, for the most part, this view of their doctrines. In treating doctrines of James and Dewey and Russell, Bradley seems, again and again, to be making concessions. Yet all he is doing is showing that he never disagreed with much of what they say, *if it is considered entirely on the level of appearance,* and not from the standpoint of reality surveying either itself or appearance. Thus he can regard their philosophies as "elements included within our view of the Absolute."

II. Let us consider first what Bradley has to say of truth as correspondence. This Bradley sometimes refers to as the absolute view of truth, for it contends that statements can be absolutely true or false, i.e., true or false apart from degree. "Within limits and in their proper place our relative view insists everywhere on the value and on the necessity of absolute judgments both as to right and wrong and as to error and truth. Life in general and knowledge in particular rest on distinction and on the division of separate regions . . . so far as we assume this, we of course can have simple error and mere truth. Thus the doctrine which I advocate contains and subordinates what we have called the absolute view, and in short justifies it relatively."[4] The "relative view" is, of course, the view of the parts as relative to the Absolute, so that no part is entitled to be regarded as itself absolute.[5]

The above seems so clearly a continuation, in the *Essays,* of the view expressed in our last quotation from *Appearance and Reality* that it is difficult for me to see how it can be supposed to be a departure. For a more explicit statement of the same position with respect to correspondence, we may look to a different section of the *Essays.*

---

[3] *AR,* p. 459f.
[4] *TR,* p. 266f.
[5] The correspondence theory, from the relative point of view, is but one possible theory of truth at the level of appearance. An instrumentalist theory is equally valid. Indeed, I think Bradley uses "correspondence" as a generic term, for he makes use chiefly of an instrumental criterion on this level, and throughout the Essays pays tribute to its power.

"If we now return to that view for which truth is a mere copy of things, we have seen that in the end no such doctrine is admissible. But from a lower point of view it may be convenient to speak of truth as corresponding with reality and as even reproducing facts. In the first place the individual in truth-seeking must subject himself. He must . . . suppress ideas, wishes, and fancies, and anything else in his nature which is irrelevant to and interferes with the process of truth-seeking. And hence in a sense the individuals can have something in common, correspondence to which is essential for truth. Secondly, in truth-seeking the individual . . . must follow the object. Our understanding has to cooperate in the ideal development of reality, and it has not, like will, to turn ideas into existences. And thus following the object the ideas of the individual in a sense must conform to it."[6] A little farther on Bradley writes, in reference to the above: "In the above senses truth may be spoken of as corresponding to facts, and it is right and proper as against one-sided views to insist on this correspondence."[7]

In the first two sentences of the extended quotation above, we may translate "in the end" as "from the standpoint of reality" (a substitution which gives the meaning of that phrase almost every time Bradley uses it), and "from a lower point of view" as "from the point of view of appearance." Then we have a statement of the point of view from which we can accept a correspondence theory of truth: that of appearance surveying itself. The possibility of error here lies in confusing appearance with reality, or, in other words, regarding the correspondence theory as explanatory of the whole, or even of a part from the standpoint of the whole. If we try to see how the same judgments are to be evaluated with respect to truth, when we look at them in the light of the whole, we find ourselves confronted with the only theory of truth Bradley developed in any detail: the coherence theory.

III. I have already discussed the theory that truth consists in coherence, as well as its concomitant doctrine, that of degrees of truth,[8] which follows from the thesis that absolute truth is the system of the whole. There are some further remarks, however, which I should like to make at this point.

The notion of degrees is regarded by Bradley as explanatory of the truth-value of all judgments within appearance when they are regarded from the standpoint of the Absolute. Since nothing is perfectly true except that which is both harmonious and all-inclusive, all else is

---

[6] *TR,* p. 118f.
[7] *TR,* p. 119f.
[8] See Chapter V, section 2.

partly true and partly false. From the standpoint of reality surveying itself all appearance may be condemned as simply false. But when appearance is seen from the standpoint of the whole, all that is false is seen to be false in degree and so true, also, in degree. The degree is determined by the amount of correction which would make the judgment perfectly true. We may regard degrees of truth in appearance as a series between 0 and 1. 0 is the impossible, the self-contradictory in a strict sense. It has no truth, for it has no meaning and no reality. 1 is the absolute. It is perfect truth which resides only in the whole. Both 0 and 1 are unattainable limits which may be approached indefinitely. The series in between is an infinite gradation, possessed of error insofar as falling short of 1, and of truth insofar as being above 0.

Throughout his writings Bradley insists that all judgment depends on conditions. The word "contradiction" is applied to any judgment which fails to include all its conditions, i.e., all its connections with the whole. And, since this is the case with every possible judgment, they are all regarded as "contradictory" and so as appearance. It is the attempt to state the conditions of judgments that forces them to pass into inference and so move on and on towards completion. Insofar as all its conditions are not stated each judgment is connected to each other judgment only externally, thus giving rise to the paradoxes of appearance. And until all conditions are made explicit every judgment is only more and less true.[9] "The growth of knowledge consists . . . in getting the conditions of the predicate into the subject. The more conditions you are able to include, the greater is the truth. But so long as anything remains outside, the judgment is imperfect and its opposite also is true. Certainly the truth of the opposite becomes progressively less, and may even be negligible, but on the other hand it never disappears into sheer and utter falsehood."[10]

IV. Although it is impossible to have absolute truth, what would it be like if we could have it, or rather, what kind of thing is this absolute truth which is forever beyond our capacities? What are the characteristics which it would have to possess which make it unattainable? These are questions which exercised Bradley's ingenuity for a period of years, but at which, though they drove him to a kind of mysticism, he never boggled. Any attempt to answer such questions involves a willingness to look at the Absolute from the standpoint of its own all-inclusive harmony.

Implicit in *The Principles of Logic,* Bradley's solution to this prob-

---

[9] See *TR,* p. 228n.
[10] *TR,* p. 233.

lem was developed and held consistently through all his later writings. Truth (with the initial letter capitalized) consists in a comprehensive statement of conditions, a system from which nothing is excluded. But here Bradley is like a theologian who insists on the infinite extension of God only to find that his refusal to limit the Almighty in any respect has committed him to the pantheism he abhors. For Truth to be all-inclusive it would have to contain that which is not ideal and so lose its proper character as truth. Yet this suicide is the proper end of truth and, even if Truth ceases to be ideal, it has attained reality. "The end of truth is to be and to possess reality in an ideal form. This means first that truth must include without residue the entirety of what is in any sense given, and it means next that truth is bound to include this intelligibly. . . . Truth is not satisfied, in other words, until it is all-containing and one."[11]

It is clear that on this level the criterion of truth is identity with reality. Both Truth and reality are to be judged in terms of the criteria of all-inclusiveness and harmony. Harmony, or consistency, might be regarded as the sole criterion of truth as system, but when that system is the whole it must be emphasized that either criterion implies the other. Since these are the criteria on which the theory of truth as coherence is based and since, further, they constitute a virtual definition of reality, it may be more obvious why I called the standpoint which regarded truth as coherence, that of reality surveying appearance. For it is, indeed, only in terms of what it would mean for truth to be absolute that the doctrine of coherence and of degrees of truth is intelligible.

Knowing what it would mean to have Truth should clarify the reasons for its unattainability. "But when we judge truth by its own standard, truth evidently fails. And it fails in two ways. . . . (1) in the first place its contents cannot be made intelligible throughout and entirely. . . . (2) And, failing thus, truth fails again to include all the given facts, and any such complete inclusion seems even to be in principle unattainable."[12] A little farther on, he writes: "Truth came short because, and so far as, it could not become that which it desired to be and made sure that it was. Truth claimed identity with an individual and all-inclusive whole. But such a whole, when we examine it, we find itself to be the Universe and all reality. And when we had to see how truth fails, as truth, in attaining its own end, we were being shown the very features of difference between truth and reality. And in passing over into reality and in thus ceasing to be mere truth, truth does not pass beyond its own end nor does it fail to realize itself."[12]

[11] *TR*, p. 114.
[12] *TR*, p. 115f.

In the end (to use the phrase as Bradley does) Truth consists in identity with the real, but in becoming the whole it ceases to be truth. This is an interesting type of mystical doctrine, avowing as its end a union with reality in which the specific character of truth is lost. It seems to follow that for Omniscience the world is not known intellectually but rather is known by being one with it, if indeed such identification can be called knowledge. This is the age-old demand somehow to grasp the actual stuff of the world in addition to comprehending its characters. And it matters not that the stuff of the world is, for Bradley, experience. Ultimate knowledge would be, in the light of his beliefs, not understanding, but being, all experience. And so it would not be knowledge at all but, perhaps, a single experience of the Whole. The fatal contradiction of his ultimate criterion of truth is that in order for anything to be true really (from the standpoint of reality) it cannot be true at all. In an admirably succinct passage in the last chapter of *Appearance and Reality* Bradley summarizes this difficulty which cannot be resolved intellectually and which leads to mysticism. "The essential inconsistency of truth may, perhaps, be best stated thus. If there is any difference between *what it means* and *what it stands for,* then truth is clearly not realized. But, if there is no such difference, then truth has ceased to exist."[13]

V. This is an ultimate scepticism which is forced on Bradley, as it would be on any honest and conscientious thinker, by the nature of his initial assumptions. Idea, judgment, and inference constitute a system in which there is no stopping place. Although Bradley did not develop a theory of meaning in accord with his theory of truth it seems clear, at least to me, that meaning would grow with the addition of new statements of conditions and that the thoroughly meaningful would be the whole. Yet when meaning reached completion it would, like truth, have to be that which it stood for, and so would not be meaning at all. Truth and meaning must remain a matter of degree so far as we have them at all (except that, for practical purposes, or from the standpoint of appearance, we may regard meaning as fixed, just as we may regard truth as correspondence.) Yet their ends are suicidal in that they must transcend the only realm in which their characters are possible.[14]

And not only do truth and meaning lose their characters in the Absolute; the entire realm of appearance is transformed. Relations disap-

---

[13] *AR*, p. 482n. I take this to mean that truth is realized only when there is no difference between the meaning of discourse and the Reality it intends, or signifies, i.e., when they are identical.

[14] "And even degree itself . . . in the end is transcended." (*TR*, p. 329).

pear, since they are contradictory, or incomplete, but so do space and time, motion and change, etc. Ultimately all appearances, all the rich colors of the tapestry of daily experience, lose their meaning and their characters. But this does not mean that in their own place none of these things has warrant. They are necessary to life and should be explained in philosophies of appearance, philosophies which are in error only insofar as they pretend to be describing ultimate things, rather than the things of finite life and thought.

2. "FLOATING IDEAS" AND ERROR

I. Bradley's definition of judgment in the first edition of the *Logic* was bound up, as we have seen, with a belief in "floating ideas," i.e., with a belief that the ideal and the real were completely separate, that discourse and reality were two things, and that ideas, which were "universal meanings," were "wandering adjectives" mentally applied by the act of judgment, now to one portion of the real and now to another. We saw, further, that in the revised edition of the *Logic* this was regarded as a mistake and that passages dealing with "floating ideas" were carefully altered. Too often this has been taken to mean that Bradley did not regard it as possible, in his later writings, for ideas to "float," or, in other words, that he thoroughly disavowed the notion that content could be severed from existence, that a content should be applied where, actually, it did not belong. This had been his first explanation of error, and, as we shall try to show, it was never given up entirely, although it was modified. Had Bradley changed his opinions so completely, it would perhaps have been impossible for him to account for error at all. As it was, he was in a position not entirely dissimilar from that of the New Realists, when confronted with the same problem.

In order to understand the relation between the ideal and the real and, finally, the way reality reveals itself in what Bradley calls "finite centres," it is important to consider his actual doctrine in his paper *"On Floating Ideas and the Imaginary,"* contained in the *Essays on Truth and Reality.*

II. The doctrine of "floating ideas" can, perhaps, be stated thus. Ideas are both psychical existences and their contents. For logic the former is irrelevant and ideas are to be understood as pure content, objective meaning. This meaning is not an existence but is an ideal entity which, in judgment, is predicated of the real. Since what is normally regarded as the subject of a judgment is as much a meaning as the predicate, the two may be taken as one idea predicated always of the same subject,[15] which is reality. A judgment may be taken as true (this is on the level of appearance from the standpoint of itself, when regarded in terms of Bradley's metaphysic) when the idea predicated of reality actually holds within it, and it may be taken as false when the idea does not hold, "hold" having the force of "correspond."

Obviously, when the account of "idea" given above is altered, a corresponding alteration must take place in the theory of truth and error. Bradley's writings, after the first edition of the *Logic* are replete with phrases like "all ideas must qualify reality," and "any idea must be real." Into the meaning of these phrases I propose to inquire in the next chapter. Here I want to try to fix the precise meaning of Bradley's disavowal of "floating ideas."

III. It was a mistake, Bradley decided, to think that all ideas were not somehow attached to the real. But if all ideas were equally real, would not all judgments have to be true or, at least, equal in truth-value? The answer that Bradley gives is that reality is composed of many worlds (here, I suppose, one could substitute for "worlds" such phrases as "universes of discourse," or "frames of reference"): there are worlds of everyday experience, of imagination, of mythology, etc. Every idea is real in one of these realms; there are no ideas which qualify nothing. Even the idea of nothing must qualify reality in some way. But every idea is not real in the realm to which we ascribe it in judgment. When the idea is real in the realm about which we are judging, it follows, I presume, that we have truth in its relative sense. And when the idea is real in a realm other than that which is the context of the judgment, we have error.[16]

For an idea to "float" it would have to be real in no realm whatsoever, and this, clearly, can never be the case on the above account. But if ideas do not "float" in that absolute sense, they still "float" relatively wherever we have error, for there they have no reality in the universe of discourse which, at the moment, is relevant. "Because there are many worlds, the idea which floats suspended above one of them is attached to another. There are in short floating ideas, but not ideas which float absolutely. Every idea on the contrary is an adjective which qualifies a real world, and it is loose only when you take it in relation to another sphere of reality.[17]

IV. If we turn from the level on which we have been discussing truth and error to that of appearance from the standpoint of the

---

[15] Bradley sometimes treats the subject as an existent and the predicate, only, as pure meaning.
[16] See *TR*, p. 250f.
[17] *TR*, p. 32.

whole, we can see more clearly what was perhaps Bradley's chief motivation in modifying his doctrine of "floating ideas." Since all ideas are somewhere real, there is no such thing as absolute error. What we predicate must hold of reality somewhere, even if not where, in the judgment, it is thought to hold. When we err in such a manner we have less truth in our judgments, but we still have some truth. By alteration we can make our judgment truer, i.e., closer to reality. ". . . there is no possible judgment the predicate of which can fail somehow to qualify the Real; and there is hence no mere error."[18]

It is this change in the doctrine of "floating ideas" that unites the theory of truth held entirely at the level of appearance with the theory of truth held from the standpoint of appearance seen in terms of the Absolute. The correspondence which distinguishes truth from falsehood on the "lower" level is, when looked at from the outside, of such a character that there is always some correspondence, sometimes more and sometimes less. Even the word "correspondence" is only used for practical purposes, for actually where the idea qualifies the real it does not do so in the sense that it is an ideal counterpart or copy of that which is not itself ideal, but rather in the sense that it is the real, ideally apprehended.

V. Even the negative judgment (and it was in terms of this shift in doctrine that Bradley revised his account of negation, in a manner which we have already treated)[19] which may be taken as denying a predicate of some object, contains, as a predicate, an idea which somewhere qualifies the real. But suppose the subject is reality itself, how can a predicate which is denied be taken as qualifying, in any way, that of which it is explicitly said not to hold? "Where the subject, from which the idea is repelled, is the Universe at large, it may be objected that we have no longer here a distinction taken within reality. The answer is that here the Universe as a whole is distinguished from its own partial contents. What we deny is that the idea, which qualifies a finite sphere within the Whole, is in the same sense true of the Whole."[20] The contention that no idea "floats" absolutely was based on the distinction within the universe of different realms; what did not qualify the realm in question was taken to qualify some other. When an idea is denied of the whole it is taken, nonetheless, to hold of some sphere within it. And to insist that an idea which qualifies some portion of the total Universe must, therefore, qualify the Universe as such, is, simply, to insist on committing the fallacy of composition.

[18] *TR*, p. 252.
[19] Chapter III, section 3.
[20] *TR*, p. 41.

CHAPTER VII

THE IDEAL AND THE REAL

1. THE IDEAL, THE REAL, AND SATISFACTION

I. The relation between the ideal and the real is a matter of fundamental importance to the structure of Bradley's metaphysic. To understand that relation is to clarify many utterances that otherwise are delphic and also to gain in the comprehension of Bradley's account of the relation of the individual to the world. There is involved, too, the notion that satisfaction is the criterion of truth, the theories of truth we have considered being an account of that in which satisfaction consists.

Bradley's language, when he writes about the ideal in its relation to reality, is always provocative. "To regard logical implication as merely 'ideal'" he writes, "is an error."[1] And in another place: ". . . implication, where genuine, is also real."[2] The language I have used in discussing "floating ideas" (language in which I followed Bradley), raised, without answering them, many questions about ideas "qualifying reality", and "being real." And this is the language Bradley uses throughout. In the revision of his *Logic*, for example, he has this passage: "There are no 'mere ideas'. Logic *must* assume that the ideal is real somehow and somewhere. The idea that did not qualify Reality would certainly fail to be an idea."[3] The assumption that to be real and to qualify reality is one thing, seems clearly to be contained in these sentences.

The questions which I shall ask are, basically, three: (1) In what sense are ideas regarded as real? (2) What is the meaning of satisfaction as the criterion of truth? (3) On the basis of the foregoing, how is individual experience related to that single Experience which is the Absolute?

II. A great deal of Bradley's language gives the impression that ideas are the objects of the real world, a doctrine that seems much like that of the New Realism when it is realized that the solution of the problem of error implied by the notion that ideas "float" relatively is in terms of frames of reference, the sort of solution one would ex-

---
[1] *PL*, p. 236f.
[2] *PL*, p. 600.
[3] *PL*, p. 237, note 9.

pect from a New Realist. On the other hand, many of Bradley's sentences clearly imply a belief that ideas are portions of some individual experience. These are not incompatible, certainly, and Bradley shows that both are involved in what he means by "idea."

The precise meaning of the word "qualify" in the sentence: "all ideas qualify reality," is very difficult to ascertain; indeed, except for an explicit statement by Bradley, it might be impossible. A may be said to qualify B if in some way it modifies or alters it. At times it seems that this is Bradley's meaning and there is a sense in which thinking makes a difference to the Universe: in that it is an event within it. It might, however, be thought that ideas qualify the real in that they, in some sense, create or alter that which is thought, but that this is his belief Bradley explicitly denies. He is far from indecisive on this point. The only difference thinking makes to the universe, he insists, is that it is an event within it and just as much a portion of reality as anything else.[4]

Bradley's explicit statement of his meaning follows: "Any knowledge which on my view can in a proper sense be called truth, is the qualification of reality by ideal content. The real must here have the form of an object, and the idea must in some sense have an existence other than that of the object. With these points I have dealt fully elsewhere and I propose to go on here to ask first as to the meaning of qualification. That meaning is derived from immediate experience and sensible perception. If you take, for instance, an object such as an apple, this is qualified by its adjectives. It is each and all of them, and yet it is something more, though you are unable to say what. It is different from its qualities, and it is also the same and one with them. This is the idea of qualification which we apply to judgment."[5]

Reflection on this passage leads, I think, first to the realization that the idea is, in some sense, its object. The difficulty in understanding just how this is the case arises, for me at least, from the fact that Bradley is not stating his meaning literally but is providing the reader with an analogy. An idea is its object in the sense that the qualities of any thing make up the thing itself; but the idea is "something more" than its object in the sense in which a thing may be regarded as more than the sum total of its qualities. It is interesting to note Bradley's use of the word "adjective" as an equivalent of "quality," since the *Logic* contains so many descriptions of idea as adjective. But there is a great deal of ambiguity in the passage. In what sense is an apple "something more" than the qualities which compose it? The

---
[4] *TR*, p. 336f.
[5] *TR*, p. 324.

answer of Locke and Berkeley was that in addition to being a group of qualities, every thing was a substance of some kind. But what is Bradley's answer? Is it possible for him to believe in any kind of substance in addition to qualities and remain consistent with his emphatic doctrine that the only "stuff" of the world is experience? The poetic Bishop of Cloyne had disavowed material substance but had explained the things in the world that were beyond finite experience in terms of an experience that was infinite, within whose reaches human experiences were like a series of perspectives. As we shall see, Bradley's answer had much in common with Berkeley's.

Another line of analysis might be employed to arrive at an understanding of Bradley's metaphor. In the second sentence of the section quoted, there occurs this statement: "the idea must in some sense have an existence other than the object." Perhaps the reason that the idea is not the object is that the idea has an existence of its own, the type of existence which is proper to a content of mind. But this is to retain the same problem within another context; we now are constrained to ask what, since the object must exist, as idea, within the mind, is there in the mental, the idea, over and above the object it thinks?

Perhaps, before attempting to answer any of the above questions, we can grasp what, apart from such answers, Bradley is saying. An idea is its object, it seems, in the same way that the qualities of an apple are the apple. To "qualify" might mean to be a quality of, and an idea, then, might be regarded as a quality of its object. This might be rendered less cryptic by saying that, since every thing is a portion of experience, its qualities are what they are perceived and thought to be. The only mistake thought can make is to assign a quality to an object other than the one which, in sensuous perception, actually possesses it. An idea, then, is not so much *a quality* of an object as it is *the qualities* of the object. This is another way of saying that, in thought, only qualities (in the sense of characteristics) can come over, and never the "stuff," whatever it may be, that is supposed to underly the thing in the real world. The idea, then, is its object insofar, and only insofar, as the object is the sum of the characteristics of a real thing. But for Bradley the goal of thought is more than this. Perfect truth would be the being as well as the content of its objects. And thus it would cease to be truth, as it would cease to be thought, by losing its ideal character.

If we ask the question: in what, for Bradley, does the being of anything consist? the answer, I think, must be: in that it is a portion of the Whole. The Absolute is ultimately responsible not only for the character of its constituents but for the reality as well. Where Berkeley would say that to be consists in being experienced, Bradley seems to say that to be is to be within Experience, i.e., within the Absolute. Though the answers seem quite different at first, many of the differences vanish when it is remembered that Berkeley meant that the total experience which was God's was responsible for all being. On the other hand, Bradley's emphasis falls on system. Being consists in participating in the system of the Whole. Total Experience is not, for Bradley, the experience of any soul (not even the experience which is God's); it is the Experience a soul would have if it could encompass all things, a single comprehensive system, within one experience. Thus thought never contains its object completely, for it never contains that in virtue of which the object has its being. Perhaps, also, it might be said that thought, being but one element in experience (even at the level of appearance), does not contain the entirety of even the experienced object, or the object as it appears.

It would follow that when Bradley revised his doctrine of "floating ideas" and insisted that an idea is not pure content apart from reality but, rather, qualifies the real, he meant that it does that by being the *actual* content, or the sum of attributes, *of the entity which is its object*. This, if we leave aside the Absolute, is a realist doctrine but, if we consider only the function and not the existence of God or spiritual substance, so was the philosophy of Berkeley.

III. Connected with Bradley's notion of the relation between idea and object is the constantly recurring, seemingly hedonistic, doctrine that the intellectual criterion, the standard of truth, is satisfaction. Sometimes he calls it satisfaction of the intellect, sometimes that which satisfies man's deepest desires. In writing of *Appearance and Reality* in the appendix to that volume, Bradley says: "The actual starting-point and basis of this work is an assumption about truth and reality. I have assumed that the object of metaphysics is to find a general view which will satisfy the intellect, and I have assumed that whatever succeeds in doing this is real and true, and that whatever fails is neither. This is a doctrine which, so far as I see, can neither be proved nor questioned. The proof or the question, it seems to me, must imply the truth of the doctrine, and, if that is not assumed, both vanish."[6]

Despite the matter-of-fact way in which Bradley states his assumption, it is far from self-evident. It seems to be a kind of cosmic hedonism which insists that the Universe must be of such a character as

---

[6] *AR,* p. 491f.

to realize man's aspirations. Unless this were so perhaps there could not be in the Absolute a balance of pleasure over pain, and he insists this is the case.[7] Bradley's assurance, however, does not serve to make the doctrine seem less implausible and it appears to have little or no justification until we examine the relation of the individual to the universe. That the doctrine of truth as satisfaction may seem far less obvious to the reader than it did to Bradley, he was forced to recognize when he wrote the papers which went to make up the *Essays on Truth and Reality*. "It is after all an enormous assumption," he writes, "that what satisfies us is real, and that the reality has got to satisfy us. It is an assumption tolerable, I think, only when we hold that the Universe is substantially one with each of us, and actually, as a whole, feels and wills and knows itself within us."[8]

The insistence that man is a portion of the Universe rather than a creature (usually regarded in this case as in essence a mind or spirit) set apart from it, is found in many writings whose authors mean little more than that man has a body. Sometimes this insistence is a manifesto to terrify those who refuse to believe that man is continuous with other biological species, but even in that context it can mean little more than that, for certain purposes, it is important to define man as an animal. Few of the writers who insist on the continuity of man with nature (Bradley would use some other word, probably the Whole or the Universe), have tried systematically to trace the implications of their doctrine. Some, at least, among modern naturalists would accept as one of these implications Bradley's belief that " . . . my desire and my will to have truth is the will and the desire of the world to become truth in me. Truth is a mode of the self-realization of myself and of the Universe in one."[9] It is in these terms that Bradley can define truth and reality as satisfaction. "What I mean by truth and reality is that world which satisfies the claim of the Universe present in and to what I call my self."[10]

IV. The implication of the above is that the Universe reveals itself (though never fully) in the thinking of individuals within it. And, if a belief in the continuity of the individual with the Universe results in a changed conception of the individual, it results, also, in a changed conception of the Universe. There are modern naturalists who will go as far as this but who hesitate to go one step farther. It

---

[7] See, for example, AR, p. 473f. The doctrine, to my knowledge, is not mentioned in Bradley's writings after *Appearance and Reality*.
[8] *TR*, p. 242.
[9] *TR*, p. 121.
[10] *TR*, p. 414.

is a delicate piece of thinking that is required and some of the conclusions are not what they would want them to be. Bradley, in any event, was not to be stopped, and he proceeded to the doctrine that "the Universe to me is one Experience which appears in finite centres."[11] This follows directly from what he means by reality and what he means by self. It is the theory in terms of which the two are united, a theory propounded in *Appearance and Reality* and treated in a little greater detail in the *Essays*.

What, we must ask, does Bradley mean by a finite center, and how does it differ from a self and a soul? The answer, to begin with, seems to be that a finite center is what we might call a perspective; it is a world experienced by a self and is not the self that experiences. Within it is even the experience of the self and, if it were otherwise, how should we know the self at all? Let us examine Bradley's language when he writes about it. ". . . a finite centre, when we speak strictly, is not itself in time. It is an immediate experience of itself and of the Universe in one. It comes to itself as all the world and not as one world among others. And it has properly no duration through which it lasts. It can contain a lapse and a before and after, but these are subordinate. They are partial aspects that fall within the whole, and that, taken otherwise, do not qualify the whole itself. A finite centre itself may indeed be called duration in the sense of presence. But such a present is not any time which is opposed to a past and future. It is temporal in the sense of being itself the positive and concrete negation of time."[12]

I am not sure that I understand Bradley as he would want to be understood but I think that he regards a finite center as a direct experience in the sense that our experience is always of what we call "the present," and our experience of the past in retrospect or of the future in imagination is still a "present" experience of them, never literally a past or a future experience. Our perspective is "the positive and concrete negation of time" in that, though the present change, develop, or unfold, it is always "now." This present is experienced as the world and it is, indeed, the Universe as revealed to the individual.

We may think of the Universe as a whole which is expressed in many perspectives, or finite centers, and which may or may not contain more than the perspectives. "The way of taking the world which I have found most tenable is to regard it as a single Experience, superior to relations and containing in the fullest sense everything which is. Whether there is any particular matter in the whole which falls out-

---

[11] *TR*, p. 410. See also p. 413.
[12] *TR*, p. 410.

side of any finite centre of feeling I cannot certainly decide; but the contrary seems perhaps more probable."[13] If there is nothing in the Universe which is not contained in individual perspectives, how can Bradley's scepticism be explained? Not as a theory which insists that there is some experience beyond finite experience. This, in any event, would entail enormous difficulties in understanding what is meant by "experience", and might have to include the notion of "the possibility of experience." Bradley's scepticism consists in a denial of the efficacy of thought in its attempt to explain what is contained in finite centers. The whole is experienced, probably in full, but that does not mean that it is understood, nor that it is experienced *as a whole*. Thought is an abstraction, an element within experience, which, by its very nature, views the Universe in terms of related parts, whereas the Universe is a whole such that within it relations are completely submerged.

V. Perspectives are, in a sense, views of a common World, but they cannot be directly shared. Communication, I presume, is an attempt to identify elements within one center with elements within another. And the experience by which each center is constituted is to be regarded as the experience of some soul. "A finite center is not a soul, or a self, or an individual person."[14] "A soul is a finite centre viewed as an object existing in time with a before and after of itself."[15] ". . . the soul is a thing distinct from the experiences which it has, which experiences we take not as itself but as its states. The finite centre is an experience which is in one with its own reality. It comes to itself . . . immediately as a content which is the Universe. And thus, when by a construction you prolong the finite centre in time, you have still not arrived at the idea of a soul. In order to reach this you must go on to distinguish the content as experienced from that which experiences the content. The latter . . . has these experiences, and yet has them not as other things but as states of itself . . . if you confine your attention to the soul as a soul, then every possible experience is no more than that which happens in and to this soul. . . . Such a conception is for certain purposes legitimate and necessary, and to condemn it while used within proper limits, is to my mind mistaken. But outside these limits what we call the soul is, I agree, indefensible. It is vitiated by inconsistencies and by hopeless contradictions."[16]

---

[13] *TR*, p. 246.
[14] *TR*, p. 409.
[15] *TR*, p. 414.
[16] *TR*, p. 415.

What Bradley means by soul is, I presume, clear enough. But why is the whole conception granted validity only within limits and what, indeed, are these limits? In terms of what has gone before, I think we may say that the soul, which is an ideal construction from the finite center of feeling, is to be considered as at the level of appearance. It is "legitimate and necessary" as everything on that level is "legitimate and necessary:" in that, for certain purposes, it is an aid to employ such a conception. It is indefensible, apart from these limits, in that all appearance is, from the standpoint of the Absolute, "vitiated by inconsistencies and by hopeless contradictions."

There is a sense in which all that is experienced is internal to a soul and may be regarded as its states. Acceptance of this notion implies no "subjectivism" on Bradley's part. Indeed, a finite center, which is the experienced content of any soul, is the real world and has such a character that it is in no way influenced by being thought. This is a doctrine associated with realist philosophy and with what has been called Objective Idealism. The states of any soul is the experienced world. And that world, at a certain level, contains things which are objects and so must contain a subject, or self.

"The self in the first place is not the same as the finite centre. We may even have a finite centre without any self, where that centre contains no opposition of self to not-self. On the other hand we have a self wherever within a finite centre there is an object. An object involves opposition, theoretical and practical, and this opposition is to a self, and it must so be felt."[17] On the level of feeling there is, of course, no distinction between a self and its objects (not-self). Such a distinction exists only at the level of thought (for it disappears in the Absolute), since thought exists only by virtue of having an object.

The self may itself be thought, thus being its own object, but it is distinct from other objects, as it is from other selves, in that it is immediately felt. "The self may become an object, and yet the self still must also be felt immediately, or it is nothing. And so felt it still belongs to that world where content and being remain, at least formally, unseparated. The self's unity with that finite centre within which and before which the whole Universe comes, remains a unity which is implicit and non-relational."[18] "My self and other selves are, each alike, constructions made in my experience. But my self is connected there with the basis of feeling, as other selves, in my experience, most certainly are not connected."[19]

---

[17] *TR*, p. 416.
[18] *TR*, p. 418.
[19] *TR*, p. 418n.

The self is the subject when we make a distinction between subject and object. Apart from such distinction there cannot be a self, and this is what distinguishes self from soul. Insofar as the soul is taken as "that which experiences the content" of a finite centre, the soul is that which experiences the self. And, when it is said that everything in that centre is a state of the soul, the self must be included. "The true relation of the self to the soul may be now stated briefly. The soul is a self so far as within that soul we have the felt opposition of not-self to self."[20] ". . . the self is a content which falls within the soul and must, I suppose, in a sense, be regarded as its 'state'."[21]

It would seem from the foregoing that the experience of the Whole, in which Truth would reach its consummation and so cease to be truth, would not be an experience possessed by any individual soul, but an experience in which the soul, like all appearance, would lose its character and become one with the Absolute. This is the meaning of Bradley's ultimate scepticism and of his mysticism as well, for only in such mystical union can truth pass beyond appearance and become Truth, which is a synonym for reality itself.

2. APPEARANCE, IDEA, AND RELATION

I. At this point it might be fruitful to ask certain questions which have, in part, already been considered, hoping that new light may illuminate some of the recesses as yet unpenetrated. I should like to inquire further, in certain respects, into (1) the relation of appearance to immediate experience, and (2) ideas as predicates of Reality, including under this heading a discussion of the internality and externality of relations.

II. There have been attempts, on the part of some philosophers, to explain the world of things and events as an ideal construction from the empirically given. Such an attempt Bradley would applaud, for he was engaged in the same undertaking. But what his philosophical colleagues, of any time, have often meant by the empirically given is a far cry from what Bradley meant by the immediate feeling-experience which he thought to be the given in experience. The notion that sense-data, the elements of sensation, are immediately experienced would be, for Bradley, the elevation of an abstraction, an element arrived at by analysis, to the position rightfully occupied by a simple experience of a whole. The origin of any thought seems to be, in Bradley's opinion, a felt uneasiness in the presence of an immediately perceived totality. This uneasiness gives rise to reflection which, by

---
[20] *TR*, p. 421.
[21] *TR*, p. 421.

the processes of intellect, seeks to eliminate the irritant responsible for it; intelligence recognizes a problem and is directed towards its solution. In the course of thought elements within the perceptual whole are discriminated and an attempt is made to understand the manner of their connection. This procedure of intelligence has, as a necessary concomitant, the creation of terms which function as principles of explanation, categories whose analysis is a task of philosophy. The categories thus employed and analyzed are the subject matter of Bradley's section on *Appearance*. The objects which these categories stand for, or which are subsumed under them, are ideal constructions from the immediately experienced whole.

The level of experience containing these constructions is what Bradley calls "appearance." It is a level never totally free from error, for it has lost a factor essential to true understanding; the whole or "configuration", the total context within which all discriminations are made. And it is because intellectual processes are essentially analytic, as well as synthetic, that thought cannot attain to a complete understanding of the experience it considers. "That which we call our real world, the past and future of ourselves and others, and the whole body of things common to us—all this in the main is ideal construction made by selection and synthesis. It is the Universe realizing itself as truth within finite centres. And the immediate experience on which this common world, so far indeed as it is common, is based, is at any time and in any centre obviously incomplete. The entire undivided Universe in short is everywhere present, but it is present as appearance and but partially. And, though it again in and for us transcends this partial character, it never does so completely."[22] By reflection on thought and appearance it is possible to understand what sort of transcendence would yield the total context without which truth cannot be complete; but it is never possible to go on to this transcendence itself, actually to grasp the whole which contains within itself every aspect of experience.

Appearance is a certain kind of experience; it might even be said that appearance is for Bradley what the name ordinarily implies: that which appears. But it is that which appears on the level of ordinary life, experience which is never immediate but which contains ever an element of judgment. So that the world as it appears in our daily living, in our sciences, and crafts, and arts, is always experienced with some form of intellectual mediation. Nothing, on this level, is experienced apart from thought, and it is that factor, indeed, which dis-

---

[22] *TR*, p. 332f.

tinguishes appearance from other levels. Bradley has two fundamental interests, culminating in two doctrines: one which might be called a philosophy of nature, and the other, perhaps, a theology. In the first he is concerned with the limited sphere of finite experience; in the second with origins and ends.[23] But the two are not kept apart. On the contrary, Bradley tries throughout his writings to clarify their relations to each other, shifting constantly in his point of view to show how one level can be regarded from the standpoint of another. So appearance from its own standpoint is essentially as it is described above. But the standpoint of the whole is more fundamental. And, seen from the heights of the Absolute, the realm of appearance is essentially that of error, a world in which content is to a certain extent (relatively) apart from the being to which it is attributed, although this can never be the case completely. This is another way of saying that ideas are never thoroughly adequate apart from the whole and that ordinary experience is always partial.

Bradley himself distinguishes the two ways of describing appearance. "The term 'appearance' has a twofold meaning. If you take it as implying an object and the appearance of something to some one then all appearance is at once both truth and error; for appearance in this sense involves a judgment however rudimentary. But the term is used also in a much wider sense, and you have appearance wherever, and so far as, the content of anything falls outside of its existence, its 'what' goes beyond its 'that'."[24] In another passage, he writes: ". . . the twofold meaning of the word 'appearance'. That sense of the term in which something appears to some one . . . is secondary. What is fundamental is . . . the presence in everything finite of that which takes it beyond itself."[25]

In terms of immediate experience, finite centres, reality, self, soul, and appearance, it is possible to locate ideas and to understand fairly well their status in Bradley's philosophy. To the question: are ideas in the individual mind or in Reality apart from the mind? the answer is: what may be called the mind and what may be called Reality are not two distinct spheres, but rather one realm which may be viewed from more than one standpoint, and inasmuch as ideas are in this realm, ideas are both in individual minds and in the real. "Error, appearance and truth . . . do not in their proper sense belong to feeling. And again in their proper sense they on our view are transcended in the Absolute. Taken as such and in their special character they be-

---

[23] Not, however, in the sense of trying to go behind experience to purpose.
[24] *TR*, p. 250.
[25] *TR*, p. 272.

long to what we may call the intellectual middle-space, the world of reflection and of sundered ideas and of explicit relations. But (and this is the point on which I wish to insist) the middle-space is not detached and it does not float. Not only do all ideas without exception qualify the Real, but ideas everywhere are only so far as they are felt. Ideas exist nowhere except so far as they belong integrally to the world of some finite centre."[26]

Ideas exist only on the level of thought and so can never be thoroughly true. But ideas are the intellectual recognition of what is felt, they are elements in an attempt to understand the "buzzing, blooming confusion" of the immediately experienced. As such they are a portion of the real world, which is experience, and so can never be thoroughly true. Error is made possible by the multiplicity of frames of reference and, though the idea must "qualify the real," it may be attributed to some sphere other than the one it actually qualifies. Finite centres are perspectives of reality which are connected with individual souls and it is in these perspectives that ideas have their being. Ideas, then, are neither psychical existences nor abstract meanings alone. They are, perhaps, what may be described as Reality cognized. And, insofar as it is cognized, it is never truly Reality, but the manner of understanding it may provide the thinker with clues to what it means to be Reality itself.

III. I should like, now, to inquire, in certain respects, into the meaning of Bradley's doctrine that, in judgment, an idea is predicated of Reality as a whole. This is a doctrine found throughout Bradley's work and one by which he seems to set great store. Yet often he seems to be thinking of a judgment as containing a subject and predicate of its own, apart from Reality. And this, at first, seems incompatible. It is the relation between these two descriptions in which I am here interested.

As far removed in time from the early *Logic* as the *Essays on Truth and Reality,* Bradley can still write: "All judgment predicates *its idea* of the ultimate Reality."[27] It is clear that any predicate must be one idea. Of course the idea predicated of Reality may be a compound idea, in the sense that, on analysis, it may be divided into more than one idea. In Bradley's example at the beginning of the *Logic* the judgment that a wolf is eating a lamb is construed as predication, with Reality as the subject, of the idea wolf-eating-lamb. But no objection can be taken to calling this one idea, since, after all, the

---

[26] *TR,* p. 268f.
[27] *TR,* p. 253, italics mine.

idea of a wolf, or that of a lamb, is itself compound of innumerable simpler ideas.

When Bradley writes of the twofold aspect of the subject, he calls one aspect the ultimate subject (Reality itself) and the other aspect the special subject. The latter may, on the account given above, be regarded as the one idea contained in the judgment, and this is the way I have chiefly treated it heretofore. But, in the light of the doctrine of error we have considered, it might be said that perhaps the special subject is the frame of reference and that what appears explicitly in the judgment is nothing more than a predicate said to hold both of Reality and of some special sphere within it. Such a construction does not fit into the frame of Bradley's language. It seems more probable that Bradley regards the content of the judgment, which is at once a special subject and a predicate of the real, as implying that sphere of Reality which is its immediate context. And insofar as the conditions of the sphere itself are not explicit within the judgment, insofar, that is, as the way in which that sphere is connected with all the others that go to make up the Whole falls outside the judgment, the idea which is the content of any judgment is, to a certain extent, not connected with its total context, and so may be said relatively to "float." This is a portion of the sceptical doctrine contained throughout the Bradleian philosophy. Although condition after condition may be included within judgments in the course of the process of inference, the ground, which is the sum of conditions and thus is Reality, can never be fully stated.

When Bradley writes of a subject and predicate explicit within a judgment, he is, I think, referring to the grammatical subject and predicate which are the terms taken by traditional logicians as being the actual subject and predicate of judgment. This he does in order that a consideration of judgment so analyzed will meet the arguments of those whom he is interested in refuting and who understand judgment in this way. As Bradley describes judgment its relations are always internal, but, when subjected to analysis, the relations are made explicit and are usually regarded as elements within the judgment rather than as abstractions created by analysis. This is an analogue of Bradley's position with respect to knowledge of the world. Whereas objects may be regarded as constructs from elementary sense-data, Bradley regards them, as has been pointed out, as selected and analyzed from an experiential whole. Just so Bradley understands the content of the judgment as one idea selected from the whole of experience rather than as a construction from the elements of terms and relations. But, from the standpoint of the total system of which it is part, even the internally related comes short, for the reasons stated in the last paragraph, of truth and reality. Judgments thought of as terms externally related may, for certain purposes, be useful at the level of appearance, being in this respect like so many other doctrines whose ultimate lack of consistency Bradley was concerned to show, but that cannot, finally, yield Truth, nor are they even properly described from the standpoint of logic.

"The ideas which we are compelled to use are all in varying degrees imperfect, and certainly this is the case with internal relations. They seek to hold on to the initial felt fact of identity in difference, and they point to a higher consummation beyond themselves and beyond all relations. But, at least in the end, they cannot, I should say, be thought consistently. On the other side external relations, except relatively and within certain limits, cannot in my opinion be accepted. They first of all seem to break wholly with the sensible fact, with that felt union of the diverse with which we begin."[28]

Internal relations, Bradley thinks, "seek to hold on to the initial felt fact of identity in difference." This means, I presume, that they are closer to immediate experience than are external relations. And the doctrine that a judgment contains but a single idea, is, as I understand it, a statement in logic of internal relations, whereas the doctrine that, in judgment, there are at least two terms united by a relation or relations, is a statement in logic of external relations. Bradley writes of internal relations that "they point to a higher consummation beyond themselves and beyond all relations" and this is so, apparently, because of the manner in which they emphasize "identity in difference." No such comment is made of external relations, which "break wholly with the sensible fact," in which there is a "felt union of the diverse." Since appearance is a middle ground bound to immediate experience while implying its own transcendence, it would seem that the doctrine of internal relations, of the single idea in judgment, is to be preferred to its opposite. But there is an element of external relations in Bradley's own doctrine. Insofar as the judgment contains a relation, some differentiation is made. The relation may be said to have entered into the terms, modifying their characters, but so long as we think of relation at all, so far, that is, as there is some differentiation which enters into the terms, that relation is entitled, to some extent, to be thought of separately. And here all the paradoxes of *Relation and Quality* break forth once more. We may say, therefore,

---

[28] *TR*, p. 239f.

that Bradley's theory of judgment implies the doctrine of internal relations but that this doctrine was not regarded by Bradley, as some critics have supposed, as utterly distinct from its opposite. On analysis of the content of the presented, discriminated whole, or on a shift in attention when considering it, internal relations are forever gone.

The understanding of a perceived whole, torn from the totality in which it has its place, as characterized by internal relations, seems to be the best way to view it in its connection with the immediate feeling in which it was first perceived and with the Whole in which it is ultimately transcended. This is so because internal relations constitute a better description of unity in diversity, of identity in difference, than do external relations. And unity and identity are fundamental characteristics of immediate experience and of the Absolute. But the realm of appearance contains sharpened difference and diversity. And external relations exhibit clearly difference in identity, diversity in unity. In a sense, therefore, the difference between internal and external relations is a difference in emphasis and degree, which is what should be expected on the level of appearance. The way in which one passes into the other, so that Bradley may be said to accept both (only within the limitation of appearance, of course), is itself an example of the union of the diverse. Bradley does not sharply distinguish and choose between the two; he regards one as the more adequate, not as the only possible. And his preference, as ever, is for an emphasis on unity rather than on diversity.

Within the sphere of appearance, viewed from the standpoint of its own limited validity, Bradley does not and can not employ his sceptical method. He is willing to discuss and evaluate the adequacy of one type of description rather than another. His choices are not, or should not be, regarded as complete acceptance of one and rejection of another, even within the realm of appearance. He must choose in terms of degree and of emphasis, and the criterion in terms of which he chooses is, ultimately, approximation to the Absolute. In other language, his choice is made in favor of that description, of whatever he may be considering, which would require less alteration to be perfectly true.

Bradley's sceptical method, which consists in denying the ultimate validity of anything that can be convicted of inconsistency, or incompleteness, is a method employed from the standpoint of the Whole. Only in terms of the Absolute is any appearance condemned and this is implied by the very method of condemnation, for what is rejected as contradictory is excluded only, in the form in which it is being considered, from Reality, which is a thoroughly consistent system. The first book of *Appearance and Reality* can thus be understood as constituting a detailed denial that ordinary experience, which is everywhere mediated by judgmental factors, can properly be considered as experience of Reality itself.

The above analysis offers a more detailed explanation of the manner in which I analyzed Bradley's treatment of relations and qualities in *Appearance and Reality*. The point made at that time was that Bradley was attacking the doctrine which opposed his analysis of judgment in the *Logic* as well as the view of the world it implied. In a sense, the elimination of what he took to be the contradictory of his own doctrine left the latter holding the field, as, at least, somewhat more satisfactory. And there was no need to go on to show that, from the standpoint of its ability to yield truth, the judgment as he understood it was in no better case. That had already been done by the limitations imposed in the *Logic* and was to be done again in the section on *Reality* by showing that truth could not be attained by the use of relations in any form whatsoever.

IV. At the very end of his life, in 1923 and 1924, Bradley was at work on an extended treatment of relations, which he did not live to finish. It is interesting to notice that he was still making the careful distinction between the relative and the absolute, between appearance and reality that characterized his previous writing. I should like to quote at some length from the fragment of his proposed article. "I will first of all consider relations, taken in an absolute sense as merely external or internal; and will then deal with the same distinction as confined to what is but relatively true."[29] Here I think "relatively true" is to be understood as that which is on the level of appearance, and "in an absolute sense" as that which is viewed from the standpoint of Reality. "What should we mean . . . by a relation asserted as simply and barely external? We have here, I presume, to abstract so as to take terms and relations, all and each, as something which in and by itself is real independently. And we must, if so, assume that their coming or being together in fact, and as somehow actually in one, is due in no way to the particular characters of either the relations or the terms. From neither side will there be anything like a contribution to, or an entrance into, the other side—or again to, or into, that union of both which we experience as a relational fact. . . . This, I suppose, is the way in which relations have to be understood, if you take them as external merely and also as ultimately and absolutely real."[30] The essence of his description of external relations

---
[29] *CE*, p. 641f.
[30] *CE*, p. 642.

is still, as it was in *Appearance and Reality,* the statement that relations, as well as terms, are regarded as independent entities of some sort, and are so regarded as a result of abstraction.

Compare with the account of external relations above, that which he gives of internal relations. "What . . . should, on the other hand, be meant by a relation viewed as absolutely and merely internal? You, I presume, still in this case would continue to take the terms each one as, so far, in and by itself real, and as independent absolutely of any whole that could be said to contain them. And you would go on to attribute to the particular characters of the terms, as so taken, some actual relation or relations which you find, as you say, to fall between them. Something like this, I suppose, is or ought to be meant by a relation which is asserted to be real ultimately and internal merely."[31] Internal relations are characterized, fundamentally, by the elimination of the relation as an independent entity. Relations are, when internal, the way in which the characters of the terms hold the terms together in some connection. But independence is assigned to the terms, that is, the terms are regarded as entities which are not dependent for their characters and, indeed, their very being, on some whole within which they are contained. This is the refusal to recognize the importance of the total context, a refusal which Bradley has everywhere condemned, and again this is the reason that he cannot accept internal relations as a true account of Reality or of those never-to-be formulated judgments which would be perfectly true.

Neither external nor internal relations can be accepted when they are "taken as valid ultimately." The argument against acceptance of external relations is virtually the same as that which we have considered in some detail, so I will not discuss it further. The argument against internal relations is what we have seen it must be, in terms of this philosophy. "Passing on now to consider relations taken as internal merely, we can reach no better result. The terms here once again are no more than abstractions. Taken each as real independently, and apart from some whole, they are things which cannot be found to exist in any actual experience. And once viewed as real, each in and by itself, there is no way in which they could pass or be carried beyond themselves so as to generate a relation."[32]

In the case of external and internal relations considered relatively, rather than absolutely, it is possible, and wise, to accept both (we are informed next). Bradley's language has proved misleading to some readers. It has seemed to them that he was, in his later writings, giv-

---

[31] *CE,* p. 642.
[32] *CE,* p. 643f.

ing up his insistence on the Absolute. He is, however, insisting on it as much as ever. He is attacking all doctrines which take as absolute anything short of the Whole. His insistence on the relative validity only of all appearance is a portion of the battle he was constantly waging on behalf of the Absolute. This may be seen clearly in a consideration of his own words. "Mere internal relations, then, like relations that are merely external, are untenable if they make a claim to ultimate and absolute truth. But, taken otherwise, and viewed as helpful makeshifts and as useful aids in the pursuit of knowledge, external and internal relations are both admissible and can be relatively real and true. And the distinction between what is intrinsic and extrinsic, or between what we call essential and (on the other side) accidental only, may not only be legitimate, but can in various degrees have genuine importance. The relations, obviously, in which a man stands, can be taken as due to his own character or ascribed, again, more or less to external facts and events. And to object to such a distinction, when confined within its proper limits, would be obviously mistaken and even ridiculous."[33]

The terms in which Bradley here makes his point are illuminating. The only way in which a term can enter into a relation is by regarding its character as somewhat modified by the relation. Yet if the relation were no more than this modification of the character of its terms, it would no longer have any being of its own and could not be distinguished from the terms as a whole. So that when terms are related they should be regarded as being modified in character by the relation, but only in some respect, never entirely. This means that each individual term is dual in nature: some portion of the term's character will enter into (i.e., be altered by) a given relation; on the other hand, there will always be a portion of the character which remains unaltered, being outside the relation, and so permitting identification of the same term as it participates in other relational situations. The distinction between internal and external relations can now be stated in terms of the portion, which will be essential or accidental, of the character of the term which enters into, or is modified by, the relation. The relation will be that portion of the terms which undergoes modification and may be distinguished, in thought, from the terms as a whole. ". . . in practice, and for a limited purpose, you can divide your individual term, and take one part as what you call 'essential'. And so far as this division is made, the distinction between intrinsic and extrinsic relations will hold. Wherever that part of your term

---

[33] *CE*, p. 645.

which you select as its essence remains outside of some relation, into which the individual term enters, the relation so far is extrinsic. And on the other hand, where the entrance of the term includes, and carries into the relation, the essence also as in one with the whole term, the relation here is intrinsic. But no such distinction, if I may repeat this, can have more than relative validity."[34]

This is Bradley's final understanding of the distinction between internal and external relations and it provides justification for a comment made earlier in the same essay: "Every relation (unless our previous inquiries have led to error) has a connexion with its terms which, not simply internal or external, must in principle be both at once."[35] He regards his conclusions here as continuous with his past writing on the same subject. And, indeed, he has merely said in another way that, essentially, internal relations are characterized by the greater degree in which the terms enter into the relation, swallowing it almost entirely, whereas, in a situation said to exhibit external relations, the relation is more independent, since the terms enter into it to a lesser extent and so do not engulf it so fully.

I do not think the final statement of Bradley's position on the subject of relations is, in any way, inconsistent with the understanding of his doctrine that I have already urged. The whole question arises from the problem in the *Logic* as to whether the content of a judgment was better described as consisting of one idea, within which the relation would be subordinate, or as two or more ideas held together by an independent relation. Since the content of a judgment is understood as an experienced whole which is abstracted from the Whole of experience, the problem turns out to be about experience. The answer is not, as it might seem, that in some situations the relation is more accurately characterized as internal and in others as external; rather the answer is that any situation may be described in both ways and, for certain purposes, one may have an advantage over the other. In any related situation, Bradley tells us, the terms are held together and, at the same time, apart, by the relations. They can never be completely together, for then there would be no relation, nor can they be completely apart, for then they would not be in any way related. This is the puzzle of the chapter on *Relation and Quality*. And on such an account any relational situation may be described in both ways.

Even on the basis of the distinction between the essential and accidental characteristics of any individual term, Bradley clings to the

---

[34] *CE*, p. 645f.
[35] *CE*, p. 641.

assertion, already quoted, that any relation is to be understood not merely as internal nor as external, but "must in principle be both at once." His justification is that any individual term is an abstraction, selected from the context of the entire experience. And there is no way of justifying, apart from some purpose of the moment, the actual extent of the selection. What is essential on some one selection might be regarded, if the extent of the selection were altered, or even if the selection were for some other purpose, as merely circumstantial. What is taken as essential is, after all, a function of selection or, given a specific selected situation, it is a function of certain purposes. So that relation, in any instance, may be regarded as either internal or external; and, if internal relations constitute a more adequate description of the wholeness of any situation, the same difficulties beset such an interpretation, in the end, as the ones which must be raised with respect to external relations. "Every term in every possible relation is due to, and involves, abstraction. And the idea that, apart from its implication beyond itself in some whole, you could possibly, starting from any kind of term, pass in any way beyond its limits is to me a radical error. And a hard division, made anywhere between what is internal merely and what is external only, together with the distinction anywhere drawn between (on the one hand) essence and (on the other hand) mere circumstances or mere matter of fact, cannot in the end be accepted. It may be justified in practice, I agree; but it cannot, I must insist, be offered as anything which possesses ultimate truth and reality."[36]

X. However any situation which can be a judgmental content is described in terms of the purposes with which we come to it, it may be regarded as a single predicate which is ascribed, whenever we think it, to Reality. In this sense there is always one idea which is the content of any judgment. On the other hand, when that idea is regarded as a special subject we are taking it as entirely on the level of appearance and, from that standpoint, we may treat it as characterized chiefly by internal or by external relations. Although characterization in terms of internal relations has a greater degree of truth, neither characterisation is really true, since both involve the conception of relation and so must remain within the realm of the finite and incomplete.

The same doctrine in the language of Bradley's metaphysics, rather than in that of his logic, would assert that any experienced thing is an element within the Whole and is dependent upon that Whole for

---

[36] *CE*, p. 646f.

its being and character. On the other hand, when the thing is considered apart from the entire Universe, it may be treated in various ways to serve a variety of purposes, but all of these ways involves some contradiction.

According to either type of statement, the sceptical implications are plain. The one idea predicated of Reality, the single perceived thing dependent upon the Absolute, is incomplete and, thus, inconsistent, when considered in itself. But its position in the Whole cannot be known until our body of knowledge is all-inclusive, a goal completely beyond attainment. Bradley's logic and his metaphysic are thoroughly continuous and the same conclusions may be derived from each. The ability to translate from one to the other, coupled with Bradley's doctrine of the finite centre, leads to the reflection that, in Bradley's philosophy, logic and metaphysics have the same subject matter and differ only in the aspects they emphasize. Discourse and appearance are aspects of an experience which is always mediated. In both can be discerned the felt background from which they developed and the outlines of the totality they imply. "We have seen," Bradley writes, "that a relational experience, taken in its strict sense, is beyond the stage of mere feeling and of mere 'inherence', and is in its essence discursive."[37]

---

[37] *CE*, p. 647.

CHAPTER VIII

SCEPTICISM AND DOGMA

I. It seems proper, at this point, to summarize the conclusions with respect to scepticism and dogma in Bradley's philosophy, which have been made in the course of this study, and then to inquire into the amount of truth Bradley accorded to his own conclusions.

II. Throughout this enquiry it has been contended that the fundamental notion of Bradley's logic (that idea, judgment, and inference constitute a system, the parts of which are mutually interdependent) generated a principle of scepticism which on application resulted in a denial of the ultimate validity of any thought or experience based on relations of any sort. The sceptical principle is what Bradley calls "contradiction" or "inconsistency." Of course in the ordinary meaning of these words, they are sceptical criteria for all thinkers, for no one is willing to accept the contradictory. But Bradley used them throughout in the sense of "incomplete," a meaning which entailed a procedural difficulty: for to condemn as ultimately invalid all that was less than the Whole, and to offer no other reason for the condemnation, would be a procedure highly dubious to most readers. Since, however, Bradley believed that the incomplete was always inconsistent (in the ordinary sense of the word), he essayed the gargantuan task of showing the specific inconsistencies in the incomplete. On the basis of his original acceptance of a system of the Whole as the sole repository of truth, meaning, and reality, he was able to accept all-inclusiveness and harmony as different emphases of the same principle. And, in the first book of *Appearance and Reality,* he undertook the exhibition of the contradictions inherent in the partial.

A great many of the paradoxes of appearance appear to me to be purely verbal, difficulties which can be removed by more precision and rigor in the statement of the problems and the terminology employed in their consideration. But a solution of these paradoxes would in no way invalidate Bradley's conclusions. The force of *Appearance and Reality* would, of course, be greatly diminished, but, in the light of the *Logic,* the worth of the total system would not be impaired. It would be enough, for a defense of Bradley, to show that everything on the level of appearance was incomplete, in that it was not thoroughly grounded. Since Truth, on Bradley's definition, can be predicated only of a system all of whose conditions are explicit, if follows that Truth can be predicated only of the Whole.

It remained to show that all appearance was incomplete, and Bradley tried to do that, not in terms of the specific contradictions involved in any appearance, but rather by pointing to the fact that appearance involves relations. That which contains relations must thereby be understood as being, to some extent, independent of all else, and hence incomplete. Should it be objected that the Absolute itself, though not incomplete, is independent of all else, the answer, I suppose, is that this is not the case, since there is nothing else from which it can be distinguished.

Bradley's chapter on *Relation and Quality* can be understood as an attempt to prove that relation implies independence of some part and that independence implies an infinite process of connection in order to become complete. The contention that relations cannot be shown actually to relate will mean, in these terms, that relation, with the independence of terms and connecting link that it implies, can not supply the type of connection in which the parts stand to each other and to the whole. So that, insofar as appearances are characterized by relations, they are but partial and their meaning, truth, and reality, are incomplete. It is because of the central character of this discussion that I confined myself to relations and qualities, during my consideration of appearance.

III. Contradiction, then, in the sense of non-completeness, is Bradley's sceptical criterion, the basis for which is the theory of judgment and inference in the *Logic*. And contradiction is the definitive character of the "middle ground" which is appearance. Stated as criterion it becomes: "the inconsistent is unreal." And by the simple process of contraposition we have the formulation: "The real (or Reality) is consistent." This, as we have seen, though a definition of Reality, is not a criterion, in that it has no methodological function. Indeed, if it were a criterion it would violate Bradley's principle that Reality is, in detail, unknowable. Being a definition but not a criterion, non-contradiction can, by its deductive development, yield only the formal characteristics of Reality. As was pointed out, the real has no ostensive reference; nor could it have, for Reality as such is never experienced.

IV. From the foregoing the character of Bradley's ultimate scepticism can be understood. It is impossible ever to have Truth, though every judgment possesses some truth and some error. From the standpoint of the Whole all appearance is error; but from the standpoint of appearance as a portion of the Whole every judgment can be evaluated (though probably with no great accuracy) as having more or less of its conditions stated explicitly than some other judgment, and so may be regarded as more or less true. In the pursuit of many interests, on the other hand, it is important to consider appearances apart from their systematic background. When we do this it is possible to have the simple truth and error which is valuable in practice. The criterion of truth on this point of view may be taken as correspondence of some kind.

In order to have Truth it is necessary to complete the system of the Whole, and so to encompass all things. But this is to pass beyond the merely ideal, for the ideal is by no means total experience, and experience is another name for all things. If the system of discourse could ever attain completion it would still not be Truth. This is a puzzling doctrine, an understanding of which, I think, is dependent upon the realization that for Bradley the content of thought is the object of thought. It is not, however, the entire object; it is the object in the sense in which the qualities of any thing are the thing. We shall return to this distinction shortly.

What must be emphasized in considering Truth is that, strictly considered, there is for Bradley no Truth at all. I do not mean merely that Truth is unattainable; I mean that there is, even as conception, no such thing. To be Truth is to be Reality, but truth is ideal and Reality is more than ideal. If one could move beyond the last possible stage of finite truth, he would have passed beyond the realm of truth. This is the suicidal aspect of the movement of thought towards ever greater completion.

Here we are confronted with a problem. On what level, from what point of view, are we to understand the knowledge of the formal characteristics of the Absolute? If we can answer this question we will know which of the three criteria of truth in Bradley's philosophy is applicable to it. Grant (as I have) that the principle of non-contradiction is arrived at by reflection on the system of discourse; that is, in a sense, from the outside. That should place it beyond appearance. But in what sense? Certainly, it is not knowledge about appearance but about the Absolute. It provides us, further, with a vantage point from which we can survey appearance and evaluate judgments in the latter realm. But it cannot itself be judged from the standpoint of the Absolute because the Absolute is not known. Perhaps it could be evaluated from the standpoint of itself, but Bradley has provided us with no criterion for such a point of view. After all, these formal characteristics were a surrogate of some sort for the Absolute and could be used as a position in terms of which appearances could be appraised as more or less true. But they are not actually the Absolute in its fullness of detail. To use language which Bradley would regard as barbarous for this purpose, the knowledge of the Absolute that is possible constitutes the definition of a class which is restricted to one member, and that one member the system of all things. But any *description* of the individual which is the sole member of that class is forever beyond thought.

Since non-contradiction and all its corollaries cannot be evaluated from the standpoint of the Absolute, what is left? We said that it was knowledge that was beyond appearance; yet it is implied by appearance. It is implied by the system of discourse and by every partial thing in the sense in which the consummation of a process is implied by the process. Our knowledge of these characteristics is the furthest reach of possible knowledge and is absolute truth in the sense that one cannot *know* more than this; one can only *be* more (if, that is, one can merge with the Absolute). Beyond this truth there can be no truth, for truth loses its character. This is the utmost that discourse can give us in the way of providing final truth.

V. The above interpretation is substantiated by Bradley's own words in his statement of *Ultimate Doubts* in *Appearance and Reality*. There he writes: "Most persons, I think, who have read my book intelligently, will credit me with a desire to do justice to scepticism; and indeed I might claim, perhaps, to be something of a sceptic."[1] Although "something of a sceptic," he is in no doubt about the truth-value of certain of his conclusions. "With regard to the main character of that Absolute our position is briefly this. We hold that our conclusion is certain and that to doubt it logically is impossible. There is no other view, there is no other idea beyond the view here put forward. It is impossible rationally even to entertain the question of another possibility. Outside our main result there is nothing except the wholly unmeaning, or else something which on scrutiny is seen really not to fall outside."[2] There is, I suppose, little question that this knowledge of "the main character of the Absolute" is what may be called a "necessary" proposition, or propositions. Of course, apart from Bradley's original postulates such propositions are far from necessary; but, granted those postulates, a denial of the chief characteristics of the Absolute will imply them, as the denial of the possibility of metaphysical knowledge implies that possibility.

In another place Bradley makes the same claim with more specific

---

[1] *AR*, p. 498.

[2] *AR*, p. 459f. It is this knowledge of "the main character of the Absolute" that I am calling "dogma."

reference to the characteristics under consideration. "That Reality is one system that contains in itself all experience, and, again, that this system itself is all experience—so far we may be said to know absolutely and unconditionally. Up to this point our judgment is infallible and its opposite is quite impossible. The chance of error, in other words, is so far nothing at all. But outside this boundary every judgment is finite, and so conditional. And here, every truth, because incomplete, is more or less erroneous."[3] Despite Bradley's strong language in his claims for the absolute truth of this knowledge of the Absolute it is not, in terms of his system, really True. Even necessary propositions are not Reality itself. Perhaps it might be said that such propositions are absolute truth but are not the proper end of the process of knowledge, for that end is to pass beyond truth and knowledge. Discourse alone can go no farther, for there is nothing discourse can do to make these propositions more complete, and so more true. Their completion would consist in passing beyond discourse into Reality.

For our knowledge of the Absolute to complete itself it would have to fulfill the condition for all completion: it would have to be all-inclusive. Bradley recognizes the modification which his claims should undergo in the following passage: ". . . in the end, no possible truth is quite true. It is a partial and inadequate translation of that which it professes to give bodily. And this internal discrepancy belongs irremovably to truth's proper character. Still the difference drawn between absolute and finite truth must none the less be upheld. For the former, in a word, is not *intellectually* corrigible. . . . Absolute truth is corrected only by passing outside the intellect. It is modified only by taking in the remaining aspects of experience. But in this passage the proper nature of truth is, of course, transformed and perishes.

"Any finite truth, on the other side, remains subject to intellectual correction. It is incomplete not merely as being confined by its general nature, as truth, within one partial aspect of the Whole. It is incomplete as having within its own intellectual world a space falling outside it. There is truth, actual or possible, over against it, and which can stand outside it as an Other."[4]

I think it is fair to say, on the basis of this quotation, that knowledge of the formal characteristics of the Absolute is to be measured in terms of the criterion of coherence. That knowledge provides the position in terms of which appearances are evaluated with respect to truth because it is the culmination of the system of degrees within which they have their being. It is the final degree of truth which ex-

---

[3] *AR*, p. 475.
[4] *AR*, p. 482f.

cludes all error. It is arrived at by consideration of the system rather than by thinking within the system because it is not a completed system of knowledge but rather a statement of the goal of that system.

In different language, the evaluation of the principle of non-contradiction and its consequences can be made as follows. What Bradley calls "the main character" of the Absolute is not only a definition of the Absolute but a theory of Truth. The question of the amount of validity to be granted to a statement of what it means to be Truth requires in answer a statement of the criterion in terms of which such evaluation can take place, and then an application of that criterion. The pragmatic theory of truth, for example, can be evaluated in terms of itself. Bradley's claim of absolute truth for his theory is based upon a criterion other than that provided by the theory. The criterion employed is that of coherence, which involves degrees of truth. Non-contradiction, which means that Truth is identity with Reality, is itself the highest possible degree of truth, the furthest reach of the purely ideal. Bradley's modification of his claim is an evaluation of the criterion of identity in terms of itself. And here the criterion falls short of Truth because it is merely ideal.

The knowledge of the Absolute in terms of its "main character" is Bradley's answer to the scepticism of British empiricism. But that knowledge is also a criterion of Truth which implies its own inadequacy. So that, although Bradley's theory of judgment and inference permits him to go beyond the knowledge of sensation to knowledge of the structure of total Experience, it also involves scepticism, though farther along in the scale of knowledge, for the total Experience whose structure is known is still beyond discourse and can be comprehended only by an act of mysticism.

The above constitutes a solution to the problem raised by Bradley when he writes of so many things that, in detail, they are not knowable. When Bradley makes the statement: "The immanence of the Absolute in finite centres, and of finite centres in the Absolute, I have always set down as inexplicable,"[5] he probably means that even a completed system of discourse would not contain the answer to such a question. Only by passing beyond the finite center into the Absolute, by becoming a single experience of the Whole, would the problem be resolved.

VI. There is still, perhaps, some question about the ultimate mysticism in Bradley's philosophy. Why is it a necessary consequence of his assumptions? Of course the insistence on all-inclusiveness as the

---

[5] *TR,* p. 246.

basic character of system was responsible for the doctrine that Truth must be identity with the real, since Truth was the completion of system and any completed system must be Reality. But the content of Reality is experience, and we may ask why Truth need be more than an experience of the Whole. The answer, I think, depends upon Bradley's doctrine of relation. The relational is always incomplete, for it contains terms and relations in some independence of each other, and so of the Whole. And to have an experience of Reality is to be in relation to it, just as knowledge of Reality implies relation to it. Further, any situation in which there is experience of the Whole involves the notion of that which experiences as, in some sense, apart from the Whole, and this is a notion at the level of appearance. So that relational situations, or appearance, cannot disappear so long as any distinction is made, so long, that is, as there are two terms. Relations only disappear when the individual actually becomes Reality. And it cannot be maintained that there is at least the relation of identity between the two, for there are no longer two. In becoming Reality, the individual, or the soul, has lost its character, There is only One, and to say that the One is identical with itself is not an expression of relationship, nor is it, strictly speaking, a meaningful statement at all.

VII. The idea of merging with the Absolute raises again the question of the relation of the idea to its object, for the Absolute is experience and the idea is, in a sense, an experienced object. Bradley urges, however, that the idea is not completely its object. In terms of the rest of his philosophy there seem to be two possible reasons for such a contention: (1) thought is but one aspect of experience and cannot pretend to contain the whole of any experienced situation; (2) an experienced situation is itself appearance and is not identical with the same situation as it is transformed in the Absolute. The first of these reasons contains, I think, insuperable difficulties. It may be granted that Bradley insists throughout that thought is not all of experience. Still, if the content of thought is not an object experienced, in what sense can an idea be said to be "real?" If it be said that the idea of an object of sense does not contain the actual impact on the senses that an experience of the object does, that is not to say that the content of the idea is something other than the object as actually experienced, including its impact. And to start to argue thus involves one in the Humean psychology with its distinction between impression and idea. Even if we use those terms the content of an idea, for Bradley, would have to be some actual impression, and "impression" would have to mean "object experienced." Thought is only a portion of all experience, but the content of thought is an experienced situation as it functions in discourse.

We must admit, I think, that an idea for Bradley is what I called it before, "Reality cognized." And, as cognized, or as ordinarily experienced, an object is a complex of relations. "Reality cognized" is not Reality; it is appearance. The difference between the object of thought and Reality is the difference between a relational situation and a non-relational Whole. Since Bradley thinks it improbable that there is any experience outside finite centers, and since he thinks that a single experience of the Whole transforms the character of objects of possible experience, we are led to conclude that the Absolute is very like a thing-in-itself, which is not beyond Experience or even beyond individual perspectives, but which is forever beyond finite experience. To comprehend the Absolute would be to become a finite center, insofar as that is a single, non-relational totality.

CHAPTER IX

CONCLUSION

I. Although I have no desire to indulge in polemic of any kind, I feel it incumbent to defend my understanding of Bradley's philosophy against an interpretation which would invalidate much of what I have written. I have treated the *Essays on Truth and Reality* as a continuation and explication of the system of *Appearance and Reality*. Yet that this is so is explicitly denied by Professor Rudolf Kagey, in *The Growth of F. H. Bradley's Logic*. It is a fundamental thesis of Professor Kagey's book that the *Essays* constitutes a rejection of the absolutism of Bradley's earlier work and the construction of a new philosophy, which may be characterized as "experiential relativism." It may very well be that I fail to understand Professor Kagey, and I confess I am puzzled by many things in his book, but the whole study seems to me to rest on a fundamental misapprehension of Bradley's meaning.

In discussing the doctrine of the perfection of the Absolute, Professor Kagey writes of "the express recantation of the *Essays on Truth and Reality*."[1] If there were an express recantation[2] there would be evidence for Dr. Kagey's thesis more weighty than any attempt to interpret specific doctrines as implying a different system of belief from that implied by doctrines written earlier. In looking for an explicit statement of recantation, one section in Dr. Kagey's penultimate chapter seems especially significant. The quotation from Bradley contained therein is also to be found in Dr. Kagey's review of the 1930 edition of *Appearance and Reality*,[3] with the comment that it is an explicit shift in Bradley's view. So that whether this is the recantation referred to does not matter; it is regarded as recantation. Professor Kagey writes: ". . . by the time the *Essays on Truth and Reality* were published, Bradley had long been departing farther and farther in his thought (if not always verbally)[4] from the absolutistic position which is represented in the

---

[1] op. cit., p. 8. I have already shown that Bradley believed in the perfection of the Absolute at the time he wrote the *Essays*. I have quoted his own words (in this study, p. 192f) and have commented upon them (in the footnote, p. 193).

[2] Professor Kagey means, perhaps, that the *Essays* as a whole constitutes recantation.

[3] *Journal of Philosophy*, 1931, pp. 137-9.

[4] Professor Kagey complains more than once of Bradley's use of language which implies already "discarded" doctrines. He explains this in one instance by saying

metaphysical basis of *Appearance and Reality*. Finally he said, 'Everywhere on behalf of the real Absolute I have been warning the reader against that false absolutism which in philosophy is to me another name for error. And it is an error which results in a twofold mistake. It takes some distinction within the whole and asserts it as being real by itself and unconditionally; and then from this misconceived ground it goes on to deny or to belittle other complementary aspects of the same whole. But, as against such absolutism, the very soul of the Absolute which I defend is its insistence and emphasis on an all-pervasive relativism.' "[5]

We have already seen that such a relativism is a consequence of Bradley's original conception of the Absolute and that the "false absolutism" against which he inveighs is a philosophy which has no Absolute as standard and so regards its own judgments about what is really appearance as absolute with respect to truth and falsehood; it is the belief that our propositions can yield "sheer truth and mere error." This Bradley denies, of logic and mathematics as well as of science and more everyday pursuits, contending that it is a result of vicious abstraction from the context of the Whole and an attitude which regards relational experience as absolute (i.e., independent of the Absolute which comprehends it in a consistent system).

Professor Kagey, as I understand him, takes the "false absolutism" of this section to be the type of absolutism embodied in *Appearance and Reality,* and the "real Absolute" to be an "all-pervasive relativism." Why Bradley refers to such a relativism as an Absolute would be a mystery but for Professor Kagey's parenthetical comment, "if not always verbally," which means, I suppose, that Bradley could not escape from the habit of using words which did not express his new thought but rather seemed to contradict it.

In order to show more conclusively that Bradley's use of "absolute" and "relative" are what I have tried to exhibit them to be, I shall quote two sections in the *Essays on Truth and Reality.* (1) ". . . there are, we may say, two main views of error, the absolute and the relative. According to the former view there are perfect truths, and on the other side, there are sheer errors. Degrees of truth and error may, on this view, in a sense be admitted, but in the end you have ideas which are quite right, and again other ideas which are quite wrong. This

---

that it "shows the essential continuity of his (Bradley's) thought." (op. cit., p. 86) But Professor Kagey thinks that Bradley's disavowal of "floating" ideas meant that ideas could not "float" at all. This, we have seen, is not the case. In any event, I think it better to believe that Bradley says what he means.

[5] Kagey, op. cit., p. 117. The quotation from Bradley is in *TR*, p. 470.

absolute view I reject."⁶ (2) "The absolute view of perfect truth and of sheer error rests, as we saw, on the idea that separate facts and truths are self-contained and possess independent reality. And such an idea (we have argued) must be rejected in the end; but this does not mean that the absolute view is to be rejected altogether. We are told (to repeat this) that to those who accept a real Absolute, and with it a relative view of truth, everything in particular becomes so much the same that the distinctions which give value to life disappear. But such a charge, I pointed out, is due mainly to misunderstanding. Within limits and in their proper place our relative view insists everywhere on the value and on the necessity of absolute judgments, both as to right and wrong and as to error and truth."⁷

In the second quotation Bradley refers "to those who accept a real Absolute, and with it a relative view of truth." It seems to me that the whole point of the use of the Absolute of *Appearance and Reality* as a standard of truth is that all truths must be relative. The doctrine of degrees in that book is merely the development in detail of what is implied about truth and error when an Absolute is accepted. The sections I have quoted make perfectly clear, I think, that the defense of a "real Absolute" against a "false absolutism" is not the defense of a "good" kind of absolutism (which is not absolutism at all, but relativism) against a "bad" absolutism (which is simply absolutism); it is a defense of the Absolute which is real and which entails relativism in its parts, against non-absolutistic philosophy which regards that which is less than the Whole as itself real, or absolute, and so denies other, equally relative, theories.

Professor Kagey's misunderstanding of *Appearance and Reality* may be seen in a typical comment. He writes of "the absolute truth of assertions about the Absolute Truth (so grimly clung to in *Appearance and Reality*)."⁸ As we have seen in the last chapter, Bradley explicitly modified his contention about absolute truth a few pages after he made it in full. Indeed, the very page on which the claim occurs contains the footnote: "This statement will be modified lower down."⁹ That modification, which we have considered, made it quite evident that Bradley denied the possibility of any absolute truth whatsoever at the time he wrote *Appearance and Reality,* a position which Dr. Kagey professes to find only in the *Essays.*

---

⁶ *TR,* p. 252.
⁷ *TR,* p. 265f.
⁸ Kagey, p. 114. I am not sure that the second occurrence of the word "truth" is not a typographical mistake.
⁹ *AR,* p. 475.

II. In the review of *Appearance and Reality* to which I previously referred, Professor Kagey discusses the change in Bradley's philosophy in the *Essays*. "The final result", he writes, ". . . is a new concept of the Absolute. . . . It is . . . immediate experience itself."[10] Throughout his writings on metaphysics, Bradley contended that the Absolute was Experience. And, as I have understood him, that Experience, could it be possessed, would be possessed in a single act of union, and so immediately. The word "immediate" might apply, also, in that the mediation of thought, all the distinctions of discourse, would be transcended in the Absolute. But Bradley used the phrase "immediate experience" in another and a specific meaning. That he retained this meaning when he wrote the *Essays* and that he still insisted that it was not Reality (although, as I have pointed out, like it in many respects) is evidenced by the following section from his essay on *Our Knowledge of Immediate Experience*. ". . . relations in fact do exist and immediacy in fact is transcended . . . the fact remains that feeling, while it remains as a constant basis, nevertheless contains a world which in a sense goes beyond itself. And when we seek for a unity which holds together these two aspects of our world, we seem to find given to us nothing but this unity of feeling which itself is transcended. Hence, as I have urged elsewhere, we are driven to postulate a higher form of unity, a form which combines the two aspects neither of which can be excluded."[11] And in another place he writes: "To myself it seems that ultimate reality is supra-relational. We find it first below relations, and again relations are necessary to its development, and yet the relations cannot rightly be predicated of the original unity. They remain in a sense contained in it, but none the less again they transcend it. And the natural conclusion in my judgment is to a higher unity which is supra-relational. In such a unity the imperfect relational scheme and the imperfect whole of feeling are both included and absorbed."[12]

I have insisted that there is a shift in emphasis from *Appearance and Reality* to the *Essays on Truth and Reality* and certainly I would not deny that through the years Bradley's thought became richer and his system more detailed. But I can see no evidence of a fundamental shift in doctrine. I think that Professor Kagey has treated the emphasis in each volume as the total philosophy contained in it. On any other assumption, I fail to understand his thesis.

I should like to quote, in conclusion, the admirable account of the

---

[10] *Journal of Philosophy*, 1931, p. 139.
[11] *TR*, p. 190.
[12] *TR*, p. 238f.

work he was doing as he conceived it, with which Bradley closed the *Essays on Truth and Reality*. "On the one hand it is the entire Reality alone which matters. On the other hand every single thing, so far as it matters, is so far real, real in its own place and degree, and according as more or less it contains and carries out the in-dwelling character of the concrete Whole. But there is nothing anywhere in the world which, taken barely in its own right and unconditionally, has importance and is real. And one main work of philosophy is to show that, where there is isolation and abstraction, there is everywhere, so far as this abstraction forgets itself, unreality and error."[13]

III. In surveying Bradley's enterprise as a whole there is opportunity for tracing the entire flow of the argument apart from its eddies and backwaters. Taken in its entirety the philosophy of the *Logic* and *Appearance and Reality* seems to be an attempt to solve the problems of British empiricism in the terms of German idealism. Ideas are no longer the "objects of thinking;" but the "objects of thinking" are ideas. They are experienced situations which function in discourse. Assuredly they are not regarded as atomic; they are, rather, an element within judgment, indeed they constitute judgment. They have in their original form no clearly discernible structure, no fixed and precise definition, but they grow and change with the development of judgment and inference. Every time, for example, the term "mutant" occurs in a biological judgment the meaning of the term is altered or elaborated. Just as an empirical generalization may become so fully established that it is regarded as a portion of the definition of that which it set out to describe, so the manifold of relations in which any term is enmeshed modifies and enriches its meaning. Experiential situations are more and more intelligible and more and more of the total system in which they participate is comprehended.

The notion that a relation must make a difference to its terms is a development of this theory of meaning, for, in a sense, all the relations into which a term enters constitute an extension of the meaning of that term. This is what causes all the havoc on the level of appearance which Bradley's analyses provide. Its denial, which is a theory of external relations stated in a crude form, provokes Bradley's argument that an infinite regression is involved in any attempt to explain it. But because some such theory is *practically* necessary, and because any theory of internal relations is in the same case in that it still clings to relations, the whole realm of appearance is condemned as *ultimately*, or theoretically, false, in terms of the Absolute, in which all relations are so internal to their terms as to be submerged in the whole.

---

[13] *TR*, p. 473.

IV. The similarity of Idealist epistemology, as represented by Bradley, to much of the neo-Realist writing on the subject is quite striking. The idea is regarded as its object, so far as that object is a part of a network of connections, or relations, which can be intellectually apprehended. There is no curtain between mind and experience, no representation of the object. It might be urged that for the Realists the experienced object is the real object whereas for Bradley Reality is never experienced. But for Bradley, too, the experienced object is real, since there is no reality but experience; it is only the Whole that evades us. The Realist insistence that thinking makes no difference to its object is a Bradleian insistence as well; experience, on Bradley's account, is not a product of the individual soul, nor of any soul—the soul itself is a logical construct developed in the course of experience. Bradley's explanation of error, in addition, is in terms of frames of reference, typical of neo-Realist thinking. Finally, Bradley's ultimate scepticism, the unattainability of the Absolute, is not too dissimilar from a Realism which finds that the subject matter of physics is beyond experience, or a Realism which regards human perspectives on the world as nature beheld or the universe of light, presumably in distinction from either nature or the universe unbeheld and unlighted. And the Idealist temper which takes the sphere of thinking to be a finite center does not seem utterly removed from the Realist temper which takes that sphere to be objective mind.[14]

V. The procedure of the section on appearance is reminiscent of Descartes' *Discourse on Method* in which all that is capable of being doubted is regarded as suspect. But there is a difference in what each thinker regarded as susceptible of doubt. In another sense the analogy to Zeno is perhaps preferable. Indeed there are many parallels in Bradley to the philosophy of the Eleatics. For Zeno the entire world of ordinary experience is tainted by the contradictions of the concept of motion; for Bradley it is tainted by the inconsistencies of relation. Where Zeno attacks, not experience itself, but experience (or physical nature) as understood in terms of the mathematical and physical concepts made current in his time by the work, chiefly, of the Pythagoreans, Bradley attacks, not Experience, but the categories, current in his time, in terms of which experience was understood, and the kind of experience which is so understood. Instead of concentrating on the concepts of natural science, Bradley places his emphasis on the categories of metaphysics and proceeds by showing their logical basis to

---

[14] Of course, differences between Bradley and the New Realists are many and of great importance. My emphasis on their similarity is due to a prevailing attitude that Bradley was completely opposed to the views of his Realist contemporaries.

be faulty. Both Bradley and Zeno are sceptics, not for the sake of scepticism, but to establish the claims of an absolutism which transcended ordinary experience. The Greek dialectician seems to have been content to rely for his dogma on his master, Parmenides, but the English master of paradox, though he inherited the outlines of his belief from Hegel, insisted upon his own formulation, and so is Zeno and Melissus in one.

The *Logic* provided Bradley with the tools of scepticism, and *Appearance* was their application. But he regarded his scepticism as having consequences for his dogma and in this he was closer to Descartes and Santayana than he was to Zeno, who proceeded as though the doctrine of ultimate units and that of the One were contradictories, so that the refutation of either was sufficient evidence for the truth of the other. The sceptical methods of both Descartes and Santayana arrived at the immediately given, the datum, as the starting-point for their reconstructions. Bradley's onslaught on current categories was more detailed and although he, too, rested on immediate experience, he insisted that the appearance upon which he had reflected implied not only its basis but its transcendence, within the context of experience.

Whereas the datum has been, for realistic philosophers, the object immediately before the mind, thus already implying the distinction of subject and object, it was, for Bradley, an immediate whole of feeling within which no distinctions were recognized. In a sense the entire concept is a product of intellectual mythology, the assumption that one can simply contemplate an object without recognizing it and without discerning any pattern, thus denying the meaning of biography. It is the myth of the given in its pristine form. But, granting such a level of experience, Bradley's acumen is immediately evident. For the simple and intense preoccupation with any object makes that object the totality of one's consciousness. The observed is, for such an observer, the whole of his experience, and the distinction between observed and observer goes wholly unrecognized. In another sense, immediate experience was, for Bradley, the material on which the categories of mind operated, the product being appearance.

Apart from the method by which such a concept was actually derived, Bradley follows more closely the Cartesian pattern. On the basis of the immediately given, the whole of the Bradleian metaphysics is constructed. Unlike the philosophy of Descartes, however, in the philosophy of Bradley the given passes into relational experience and that in turn into the Absolute. Instead of constructing one realm on the foundation of immediate experience, Bradley constructs two, the first of which implies the second. He does not return to his starting-place, his destination is not the port from which he embarked upon his intellectual journey. He is in search of a perfect city which he knows he can never reach, and he must, perforce, be content with describing it from a distance so great that the masses only are apparent, not the details. And the conditions of the adventure are such that could he ever reach the far-off city, which is impossible, he would seem to be, not a citizen within its walls, but, so great is his longing, one possessed of the city, and so, in a sense, would become the city itself.